LEADING WITH EMPATHY

WHY TEAMS THRIVE WHEN LEADERS CARE

JIM C. WATT.

Copyright © 2024 by JIM C. WATT.

All rights reserved. No part of this publication may be reproduced, distributed, or transmitted in any form or by any means, including photocopying, recording, or other electronic or mechanical methods, without the prior written permission of the publisher, except in the case of brief quotations embodied in critical reviews and certain other non-commercial uses permitted by copyright law.

TABLE OF CONTENTS

CHAPTER ONE
INTRODUCTION TO EMPATHETIC LEADERSHIP

CHAPTER TWO
THE SCIENCE BEHIND EMPATHY

CHAPTER THREE
DEVELOPING EMPATHY AS A LEADERSHIP SKILL

CHAPTER FOUR
THE IMPACT OF EMPATHY ON ORGANIZATIONAL SUCCESS

CHAPTER FIVE
CHALLENGES OF PRACTICING EMPATHY IN LEADERSHIP

CHAPTER SIX
TOOLS AND TECHNIQUES FOR DEVELOPING EMPATHY IN LEADERSHIP

CHAPTER SEVEN
CASE STUDIES OF EMPATHETIC LEADERSHIP IN ACTION

CHAPTER EIGHT
CULTIVATING EMPATHY AS A LEADER – PRACTICAL STRATEGIES FOR DAILY LEADERSHIP

CHAPTER NINE

EMBEDDING EMPATHY INTO ORGANIZATIONAL CULTURE

CHAPTER TEN
SUSTAINING EMPATHY IN LEADERSHIP AND ORGANIZATIONAL GROWTH

CHAPTER ELEVEN
CREATING A LEGACY OF EMPATHY IN LEADERSHIP

CHAPTER TWELVE
THE FUTURE OF EMPATHETIC LEADERSHIP: GLOBAL PERSPECTIVES AND EMERGING TRENDS

CONCLUSION
EMBRACING THE POWER OF EMPATHETIC LEADERSHIP

CHAPTER ONE

INTRODUCTION TO EMPATHETIC LEADERSHIP

Defining Empathy in Leadership

Empathy is the ability to understand and share the feelings of others, placing oneself in another's position to gain deeper insights into their emotions, needs, and perspectives. In the context of leadership, empathy goes beyond simply listening or offering emotional support. It is about actively engaging with team members, understanding their concerns, motivations, and challenges, and using that understanding to guide actions, decisions, and interactions.

Empathetic leadership has gained prominence in recent years as businesses and organizations have begun to realize that leaders who genuinely care about their employees foster greater loyalty, innovation, and productivity. At its core, empathetic leadership means prioritizing the well-being and emotional health of your team members, acknowledging their humanity, and treating them as more than just resources for achieving organizational goals. It transforms the traditional power dynamics in leadership, where leaders may have once been seen primarily as authority figures who gave orders and expected results. Instead, empathy allows for a more collaborative, inclusive approach that nurtures individual and collective growth.

Empathy in leadership doesn't mean coddling employees or avoiding difficult decisions; it's about having the awareness to understand how decisions affect others and using that understanding to make better, more thoughtful choices. This often requires a balance between meeting business objectives and considering the emotional well-being of the team. Leaders who can master this balance are more likely to build trust and foster long-term success.

The Importance of Emotional Intelligence

Closely tied to empathy is the concept of **Emotional Intelligence (EI)**, a term popularized by psychologist Daniel Goleman in the 1990s. Emotional intelligence refers to the ability to recognize, understand, and manage one's own emotions, as well as the emotions of others. In leadership, a high level of emotional intelligence is critical because it enhances a leader's ability to connect with their team on a deeper level.

Emotional intelligence is often broken down into five major components:

1. **Self-awareness:** The ability to notice and comprehend your own emotions and how they affect your ideas and conduct. Leaders with strong self-awareness are better equipped to manage their own emotions and respond thoughtfully to challenges.
2. **Self-regulation:** This is the ability to control or redirect disruptive emotions and impulses and to think before acting. Leaders who can self-regulate tend to be more consistent in their behavior, earning the trust and respect of their teams.
3. **Motivation:** Leaders with a high degree of emotional intelligence are driven by a passion for

their work and the ability to inspire and motivate their teams. They are committed to the success of their organizations and the personal growth of their employees.
4. **Empathy:** As noted earlier, empathy is about understanding the emotional needs of others and responding in ways that show compassion and care. It allows leaders to build deep connections with their teams, fostering trust and loyalty.
5. **Social skills:** Leaders with strong social skills are good at managing relationships, resolving conflicts, and building networks. They are effective communicators who can navigate complex social situations with ease.

Incorporating emotional intelligence into leadership allows for a more nuanced, adaptive approach to managing people. Leaders with high emotional intelligence are not only more effective at understanding and motivating their teams, but they also tend to be better problem solvers and decision-makers because they are able to take into account the emotional factors that influence behavior.

Why Empathy Matters in the Modern Workplace

The workplace has undergone significant changes in recent years, with shifts towards more collaborative, flexible, and inclusive environments. These changes have been driven by a combination of factors, including the rise of remote and hybrid work models, increasing diversity in the workforce, and a growing recognition of the importance of work-life balance. In this context, empathy has become an essential skill for leaders.

The traditional top-down, command-and-control leadership style, where leaders made decisions in isolation and imposed them on their teams, is increasingly seen as ineffective. In today's workplace, employees are looking for leaders who are approachable, open to feedback, and capable of understanding their needs. Empathetic leaders are more likely to create environments where employees feel valued, respected, and empowered to contribute their best work.

Moreover, the rise of knowledge work, where creativity and problem-solving are critical to success, has made it even more important for leaders to cultivate empathy. Unlike repetitive or routine tasks, knowledge work often requires a high degree of collaboration, communication, and emotional engagement. When employees feel that their leaders genuinely care about them, they are more likely to be engaged, motivated, and willing to go the extra mile.

Empathy fosters trust. Trust is the foundation of any successful team, and without it, collaboration, innovation, and productivity can suffer. When leaders demonstrate empathy, they show that they care about their employees' well-being, which in turn builds trust. Employees who trust their leaders are more likely to be open, honest, and willing to take risks, knowing that their leaders have their backs.

Additionally, empathy helps leaders navigate the complexities of the modern, diverse workforce. Today's employees come from a wide range of backgrounds, cultures, and experiences, and they bring different perspectives and needs to the table. Leaders who can empathize with their team members are better equipped to understand and appreciate these differences, creating an inclusive workplace where everyone feels that they belong.

Overview of Key Leadership Theories

Empathetic leadership is not a standalone concept but is deeply connected to several well-established leadership theories that emphasize human-centered approaches. Understanding these theories helps contextualize empathy within the broader landscape of leadership.

1. **Transformational Leadership:** Transformational leadership is a theory that focuses on inspiring and motivating followers to achieve extraordinary outcomes by connecting with their intrinsic motivations and values. Leaders who adopt this style are often charismatic, visionary, and deeply concerned with the growth and development of their team members. Empathy is a key component of transformational leadership because it enables leaders to understand the individual aspirations and challenges of their team members, allowing them to provide personalized support and inspiration.
2. **Servant Leadership:** Servant leadership, first introduced by Robert Greenleaf in the 1970s, is a leadership philosophy that emphasizes the leader's role as a servant to their followers. The servant leader prioritizes the needs of their team above their own and works to empower and uplift them. Empathy is a cornerstone of servant leadership, as it requires leaders to be deeply attuned to the

emotional and psychological needs of their team members. A servant leader listens, supports, and fosters a culture of care, which in turn enhances team performance and well-being.

3. **Authentic Leadership:** Authentic leadership is based on the principle that leaders should be true to themselves and lead with integrity, transparency, and honesty. Authentic leaders build strong relationships with their team members by being open and genuine, and empathy plays a critical role in this process. Authentic leaders recognize the importance of understanding the emotions and experiences of their team members, which allows them to build deeper connections and trust. Empathy in authentic leadership is about seeing the human side of each team member and responding with compassion and care.

4. **Emotional Leadership:** Emotional leadership, a concept derived from emotional intelligence theory, emphasizes the role of emotions in leadership effectiveness. Leaders who are emotionally intelligent are able to create positive emotional climates within their teams, which enhances team morale, motivation, and collaboration. Empathy is central to emotional leadership because it allows leaders to be attuned to the emotional states of their team members and respond in ways that foster a supportive and positive work environment.

5. **Situational Leadership:** Situational leadership is a flexible, adaptive approach to leadership that suggests there is no single best way to lead. Instead, leaders should adjust their style based on the needs of their team members and the specific situation they are facing. Empathy is a key skill in

situational leadership because it enables leaders to accurately assess the emotional and developmental needs of their team members and adjust their approach accordingly. Whether providing more hands-on support or giving team members more autonomy, empathetic leaders are able to tailor their leadership style to suit the situation.

The Shift Toward Empathy-Driven Leadership

The increasing emphasis on empathy in leadership reflects broader changes in societal values and expectations. In the past, leadership was often associated with traits such as authority, strength, and decisiveness, while empathy was seen as a "soft" skill that was less relevant to achieving business outcomes. However, this perspective has shifted as more organizations recognize the importance of employee well-being, mental health, and emotional engagement in driving success.

The COVID-19 pandemic, in particular, accelerated the shift toward empathy-driven leadership. As millions of employees faced unprecedented challenges, including health concerns, remote work, and caregiving responsibilities, leaders were called upon to demonstrate empathy like never before. Those who responded with compassion, flexibility, and understanding were able to maintain morale and productivity during a time of crisis. The pandemic revealed that empathy is not a luxury in leadership but a necessity, especially in times of uncertainty and change.

Empathetic leadership is not just a buzzword or trend; it represents a fundamental shift in how we understand and practice leadership in the modern workplace. By prioritizing empathy, leaders can build stronger, more trusting relationships with their teams, foster higher levels of engagement and innovation, and create environments where employees feel valued and supported. The importance of empathy in leadership is supported by a growing body of research and theory, and it will continue to be a key factor in shaping the future of leadership.

CHAPTER TWO

THE SCIENCE BEHIND EMPATHY

Empathy, at its core, is the ability to perceive, understand, and relate to the emotions and experiences of others. It allows individuals to step outside of their own perspectives and connect with the inner worlds of those around them. In leadership, empathy enables leaders to build stronger, more resilient teams by fostering trust, understanding, and cooperation. To fully grasp the power of empathy in leadership, it's essential to understand the science behind it—how empathy is rooted in biology, psychology, and social behavior, and how it influences individual and group dynamics in profound ways.

Understanding Empathy from a Psychological Perspective

Empathy is often categorized into two main types: **cognitive empathy** and **emotional empathy**.

- **Cognitive empathy** refers to the ability to understand someone else's thoughts and feelings from an intellectual standpoint. This type of empathy involves recognizing and comprehending the emotional states of others without necessarily feeling those emotions yourself. It allows leaders to analyze a situation and make informed decisions based on how others might feel or react.
- **Emotional empathy**, also known as affective empathy, involves feeling what another person is experiencing on an emotional level. When leaders practice emotional empathy, they not only

understand their team members' emotions but also feel a sense of connection to those emotions. This deeper emotional engagement is often what drives compassionate actions.

In addition to these two types, some psychologists also refer to **compassionate empathy**. This involves not only understanding and feeling another's emotions but also being motivated to take action to help alleviate distress or improve the situation. Compassionate empathy is the form most closely associated with effective leadership, as it moves beyond passive understanding and into active support.

Empathy is a psychological process that engages multiple cognitive and emotional pathways. It relies on a combination of factors, including self-awareness, emotional regulation, and social awareness. Leaders who possess high levels of empathy are not only able to perceive others' emotions but are also adept at managing their own emotional responses to maintain a calm, supportive presence in high-stress situations.

The Biological Basis of Empathy

Empathy is not just a psychological phenomenon; it is also deeply rooted in biology. Advances in neuroscience have shed light on how the brain processes empathy and the neural mechanisms that underpin this crucial human ability.

1. **Mirror Neurons**: One of the key discoveries in the study of empathy is the existence of mirror neurons. First identified in the 1990s, mirror

neurons are specialized cells in the brain that activate when we observe others performing an action or experiencing an emotion. For example, when we see someone smiling, our mirror neurons may trigger similar neural activity as if we were smiling ourselves. This neural mirroring helps us understand and empathize with the emotions of others, even when we are not directly experiencing the same feelings.

In the context of leadership, mirror neurons play a vital role in how leaders connect with their teams. When a leader demonstrates calmness, positivity, or empathy, their team members' mirror neurons may respond by triggering similar emotional states, creating a ripple effect of positive emotions throughout the group. Conversely, if a leader exhibits stress, anger, or frustration, these negative emotions can be mirrored by the team, leading to a tense and unproductive environment.

2. **Oxytocin and Empathy**: Another important biological factor in empathy is oxytocin, often referred to as the "love hormone" or "bonding hormone." Oxytocin is released in response to social bonding and plays a crucial role in promoting trust, connection, and empathy. Studies have shown that higher levels of oxytocin in the brain can enhance empathetic behavior and increase the likelihood of helping others.

In leadership, fostering strong, empathetic connections with team members can stimulate the release of oxytocin, thereby strengthening trust and cooperation within the team. Leaders who create environments where team members feel safe, supported, and valued can enhance oxytocin production, leading to stronger interpersonal bonds and more cohesive team dynamics.

3. **The Role of the Prefrontal Cortex**: The **prefrontal cortex**, a region of the brain associated with higher cognitive functions such as decision-making, emotional regulation, and social behavior, is also crucial for empathy. The prefrontal cortex helps us process complex social situations, weigh the emotional impact of our decisions on others, and exercise self-control in emotionally charged situations. This region of the brain allows leaders to take a step back and reflect on how their words and actions will affect their team members.

   Effective empathetic leadership requires a well-functioning prefrontal cortex, as leaders must constantly navigate the emotional needs of their teams while making decisions that align with organizational goals. Leaders who engage their prefrontal cortex are more likely to pause and consider the feelings of others before reacting, which leads to more thoughtful and compassionate leadership.

How Empathy Affects Brain Function and Behavior

Empathy not only influences how we perceive others but also impacts our own brain function and behavior. Research shows that practicing empathy can enhance various aspects of brain health and lead to positive behavioral outcomes.

1. **Enhanced Emotional Regulation**: Leaders who regularly engage in empathetic behavior are often better at regulating their own emotions. By understanding and connecting with the emotions of others, leaders can gain perspective on their own emotional responses, which can help them remain calm and composed during stressful situations. This enhanced emotional regulation allows empathetic leaders to handle conflicts and challenges more effectively, as they are less likely to be overwhelmed by their own emotions.
2. **Increased Social Cohesion**: Empathy fosters social cohesion by creating a sense of belonging and trust within a group. When leaders demonstrate empathy, they signal to their team members that they are valued and respected. This, in turn, strengthens the bonds between team members and promotes a sense of unity and purpose. Teams that experience high levels of social cohesion are more likely to collaborate effectively, support one another, and achieve shared goals.
3. **Improved Problem-Solving Skills**: Empathy enhances problem-solving skills by encouraging leaders to consider multiple perspectives. When leaders are able to step into the shoes of others, they gain a broader understanding of the challenges at hand and can come up with more creative and effective solutions. This is particularly important in diverse teams, where different individuals may have unique insights and

experiences that can contribute to solving complex problems.

4. **Increased Altruistic Behavior**: Research has shown that empathy is closely linked to altruistic behavior—actions that are motivated by a desire to help others without expecting anything in return. When leaders practice empathy, they are more likely to engage in altruistic acts such as offering support to struggling team members, providing mentorship, or making decisions that benefit the greater good rather than just their own interests. These acts of kindness not only strengthen relationships within the team but also contribute to a positive organizational culture.

The Connection between Empathy and Team Dynamics

Empathy plays a central role in shaping team dynamics, influencing how individuals interact with one another and how the team functions as a whole. Leaders who demonstrate empathy can create a more harmonious, productive, and resilient team environment. There are several ways in which empathy impacts team dynamics:

1. **Fostering Open Communication**: Empathy encourages open communication by creating a safe space for team members to express their thoughts, concerns, and emotions. When leaders listen empathetically, they signal to their team members that their voices are heard and valued. This openness helps to break down barriers and allows for more honest, transparent dialogue. Teams that

communicate openly are better able to address issues, share ideas, and collaborate effectively.
2. **Promoting Psychological Safety**: Psychological safety is the belief that one can speak up, make mistakes, or take risks without fear of retribution or embarrassment. Empathetic leaders foster psychological safety by demonstrating understanding and compassion when team members make errors or face challenges. When employees feel psychologically safe, they are more likely to take creative risks, offer innovative solutions, and contribute to the team's success without fear of judgment.
3. **Enhancing Collaboration**: Empathy promotes collaboration by helping team members understand and appreciate each other's strengths, weaknesses, and perspectives. When leaders encourage empathy within the team, individuals are more likely to support one another and work together toward shared goals. Empathy helps to bridge gaps between diverse team members, facilitating more effective collaboration and reducing conflicts that may arise from misunderstandings or differences in communication styles.
4. **Reducing Conflict**: While conflict is inevitable in any team setting, empathy can help to reduce the intensity and duration of conflicts by fostering mutual understanding and respect. Leaders who approach conflicts with empathy are better able to de-escalate tensions and find resolutions that address the underlying emotional needs of all parties involved. By acknowledging and validating the emotions of their team members, empathetic

leaders can prevent minor disagreements from escalating into larger, more disruptive conflicts.

Studies on Empathy and Leadership Outcomes

Numerous studies have demonstrated the positive effects of empathy on leadership outcomes, providing empirical support for the idea that empathetic leaders are more effective in driving team success. Some key findings from this research include:

1. **Empathy and Employee Engagement**: A study conducted by the Center for Creative Leadership found that leaders who exhibit empathy are more likely to have highly engaged employees. The study showed that when leaders demonstrate empathy, their employees are more likely to feel valued, motivated, and committed to their work. High levels of employee engagement are associated with increased productivity, creativity, and job satisfaction.
2. **Empathy and Organizational Performance**: Research from Harvard Business Review found that organizations with empathetic leaders tend to outperform their competitors. Empathy in leadership is linked to improved employee retention, better customer service, and higher levels of innovation. The study also found that empathetic leaders are more effective at navigating organizational change, as they are able to build trust and resilience within their teams during times of uncertainty.
3. **Empathy and Conflict Resolution**: Studies have shown that empathetic leaders are more successful

at resolving conflicts within their teams. By understanding the emotional needs and perspectives of all parties involved, empathetic leaders are better equipped to mediate disputes and find solutions that satisfy everyone. This leads to more harmonious team dynamics and reduces the negative impact of conflict on team performance.
4. **Empathy and Leadership Effectiveness**: A meta-analysis of leadership studies found that empathy is one of the strongest predictors of leadership effectiveness. Leaders who score high in empathy are more likely to inspire trust, loyalty, and cooperation from their team members. These leaders are also more likely to be seen as fair, approachable, and emotionally intelligent, all of which contribute to their overall success.

The science of empathy reveals that it is not only a psychological and emotional skill but also a biological and neurological process that plays a crucial role in leadership. Empathetic leaders are better equipped to build trust, foster collaboration, and create a positive, supportive work environment. By understanding the cognitive, emotional, and biological mechanisms behind empathy, leaders can enhance their ability to connect with their teams and drive success in both individual and organizational outcomes.

CHAPTER THREE

DEVELOPING EMPATHY AS A LEADERSHIP SKILL

While empathy may seem like an innate quality that some leaders possess and others do not, the truth is that empathy can be developed and cultivated with conscious effort. Leaders who wish to lead with empathy can hone this skill through deliberate practice, self-reflection, and a commitment to understanding and connecting with the emotions and perspectives of others. In this chapter, we will explore practical strategies for developing empathy as a leadership skill, as well as how to overcome common barriers to empathy in leadership. Additionally, we will examine how leaders can create a culture of empathy within their teams and organizations.

The Importance of Self-Awareness in Empathetic Leadership

The first step in developing empathy as a leader is cultivating **self-awareness**. Self-awareness refers to the ability to recognize and understand your own emotions, thoughts, and behaviors, and how they impact others. Leaders who are self-aware are better equipped to manage their emotional responses, recognize their biases, and be present in their interactions with others.

1. **Emotional Self-Awareness**: Emotional self-awareness is the foundation of empathetic leadership. It involves being in tune with your own emotions and understanding how they influence your behavior and decision-making. Leaders who are emotionally self-aware can recognize when

they are feeling stressed, frustrated, or anxious, and take steps to manage these emotions before they negatively affect their interactions with team members.

To develop emotional self-awareness, leaders can practice mindfulness techniques such as meditation, deep breathing, or journaling. These practices help leaders become more attuned to their internal emotional states and provide them with the tools to regulate their emotions in real-time. Additionally, seeking feedback from trusted colleagues or mentors can help leaders gain insight into how their emotions and behaviors are perceived by others.

2. **Recognizing Personal Biases**: Everyone has biases—conscious or unconscious—that shape how they view the world and interact with others. These biases can influence a leader's ability to empathize with team members, particularly those from different backgrounds or with different perspectives. For example, a leader may unconsciously favor employees who share similar experiences or values, while overlooking the needs and concerns of those who differ.

To develop empathy, leaders must actively work to recognize and overcome their biases. This requires a commitment to continuous learning and self-reflection. Leaders can start by engaging in diversity and inclusion training, seeking out perspectives that challenge their own, and regularly questioning their assumptions. By confronting their biases, leaders can broaden their understanding of others and create a more inclusive, empathetic leadership style.

3. **Practicing Active Listening**: One of the most effective ways to develop empathy is through active listening.
Active listening is a communication approach that entails fully focusing on the speaker, understanding their message, and responding carefully. It requires leaders to be present in the moment and to listen without judgment or distraction.

Active listening goes beyond simply hearing the words that are being spoken; it involves paying attention to nonverbal cues such as body language, tone of voice, and facial expressions. Leaders who practice active listening are better able to understand the emotions and motivations behind what their team members are saying, which allows them to respond with greater empathy and insight.

To improve active listening skills, leaders can practice the following techniques:

- **Maintain eye contact** and focus on the speaker without interrupting.
- **Paraphrase or summarize** what the speaker has said to ensure understanding.
- Ask **open-ended questions** to encourage the speaker to elaborate on their thoughts and feelings.

- **Reflect on emotions** by acknowledging the speaker's feelings and validating their experience.

The Role of Emotional Regulation in Empathetic Leadership

Empathy is not just about understanding the emotions of others; it is also about managing your own emotions in a way that allows you to respond thoughtfully and compassionately.
This is where controlling one's emotions is important.
Emotional regulation refers to the ability to control and manage your emotional responses, especially in stressful or challenging situations.

1. **Staying Calm Under Pressure**: Leaders are often faced with high-pressure situations where emotions can run high. Whether it's a tight deadline, a conflict between team members, or a difficult decision, leaders must be able to remain calm and composed in the face of adversity. Emotional regulation allows leaders to manage their own stress and frustration so that they can respond with empathy and clarity rather than reacting impulsively.

   To improve emotional regulation, leaders can practice techniques such as deep breathing, progressive muscle relaxation, or visualization. These techniques help to activate the body's relaxation response, reducing the intensity of negative emotions and allowing leaders to approach situations with a clear mind.

2. **Responding Rather Than Reacting**: One of the key aspects of emotional regulation is learning to respond to situations thoughtfully rather than reacting impulsively. When leaders react based on their immediate emotions, they may say or do things that escalate the situation or alienate team members. By contrast, leaders who regulate their emotions are able to take a step back, consider the needs and feelings of others, and respond in a way that promotes understanding and resolution.

   Leaders can practice emotional regulation by developing a habit of **pausing** before responding in emotionally charged situations. Taking a moment to breathe, reflect, and assess the situation can help leaders choose a response that is grounded in empathy and aligned with their leadership values.

3. **Managing Emotional Contagion**: Emotional contagion refers to the phenomenon in which people "catch" the emotions of those around them. In leadership, emotional contagion is particularly important because leaders set the emotional tone for their teams. If a leader is stressed, anxious, or frustrated, these emotions can spread to the team and negatively affect morale and productivity. On the other hand, when leaders project calmness, positivity, and empathy, these emotions can create a more supportive and collaborative team environment.

   Leaders can manage emotional contagion by being mindful of their emotional expressions and how they may impact the team. Practicing emotional regulation not only benefits the leader but also helps to create a more emotionally stable and empathetic team culture.

Overcoming Barriers to Empathy in Leadership

While empathy is a valuable leadership skill, there are several barriers that can make it challenging for leaders to practice empathy consistently. Understanding and addressing these barriers is essential for developing empathetic leadership.

1. **Time Constraints**: One of the most common barriers to empathy in leadership is the perception that there isn't enough time to connect with team members on an emotional level. In fast-paced work environments, leaders may feel pressured to prioritize tasks, deadlines, and goals over the emotional needs of their team. However, neglecting empathy can lead to disengagement, burnout, and decreased productivity in the long run.

   To overcome this barrier, leaders must recognize that empathy is not a time-consuming task but rather an integral part of effective leadership. Simple actions such as checking in with team members, offering support, and listening attentively can make a significant difference without requiring a large time investment. Additionally, leaders can schedule regular one-on-one meetings with team members to foster open communication and build stronger relationships.

2. **Emotional Exhaustion**: Leaders may experience emotional exhaustion, especially if they are constantly dealing with the emotions and challenges of their team members. Empathy requires emotional energy, and over time, leaders may feel drained or overwhelmed by the emotional demands of their role.

   To avoid emotional exhaustion, leaders must prioritize **self-care** and **emotional boundaries**. This means recognizing when they need to take a break, delegate tasks, or seek support from colleagues or mentors. It's important for leaders to practice empathy for themselves as well as for others, ensuring that they have the emotional resources to lead effectively.

3. **Cultural and Social Differences**: Leaders often work with diverse teams composed of individuals from different cultural, social, and professional backgrounds. These differences can present challenges to empathy, as leaders may struggle to understand the unique experiences and perspectives of their team members.

   To overcome this barrier, leaders must be committed to **cultural competence** and **diversity awareness**. This involves educating themselves about different cultural norms, values, and communication styles, as well as being open to learning from their team members' experiences. Leaders who embrace diversity and seek to understand the unique needs of their team members are better able to practice empathy in a way that is inclusive and respectful.

4. **Fear of Vulnerability**: Some leaders may hesitate to practice empathy because they associate it with vulnerability. Empathy requires leaders to open themselves up to the emotions of others, which can feel uncomfortable or risky. Additionally, leaders may fear that showing empathy will make them appear weak or overly emotional in the eyes of their team.

To overcome this barrier, leaders must shift their mindset about vulnerability. Far from being a weakness, vulnerability is a strength that allows leaders to build deeper connections with their team members. When leaders demonstrate empathy and vulnerability, they create an environment of trust and authenticity, where team members feel safe to share their own emotions and challenges. This, in turn, strengthens the team's emotional resilience and overall performance.

Practical Strategies for Cultivating Empathy in Leadership

Now that we have explored the challenges and barriers to empathy, let's turn to practical strategies that leaders can use to cultivate empathy in their leadership practice.

1. **Seek to Understand Before Being Understood**: A key principle of empathetic leadership is the idea that leaders should prioritize understanding the perspectives and emotions of

their team members before imposing their own views. This means approaching conversations with an open mind and a genuine curiosity about the other person's experience. Leaders who seek to understand first are better equipped to offer support, guidance, and solutions that are aligned with their team members' needs.

One way to practice this principle is by asking **open-ended questions** that encourage team members to share more about their thoughts and feelings.
For instance, rather than enquiring as to whether the choice was acceptable?" a leader might ask, "How do you feel about this decision, and is there anything you would like to add or discuss further?"

2. **Practice Empathy in Everyday Interactions**: Empathy is not reserved for crisis situations or difficult conversations; it should be practiced in everyday interactions. Leaders can cultivate empathy by consistently showing interest in their team members' well-being, acknowledging their emotions, and offering support when needed.

Simple gestures such as greeting team members warmly, expressing appreciation for their work, or offering a listening ear during challenging times can have a profound impact on team morale and cohesion. Leaders should also be attentive to nonverbal cues, such as body language and facial expressions, as these can provide valuable insight into how team members are feeling.

3. **Model Empathy for the Team**: Leaders set the tone for their teams, and when they model empathetic behavior, it encourages team members to do the same. Leaders can model empathy by being transparent about their own emotions, showing vulnerability when appropriate, and demonstrating compassion in their interactions with others.

   For example, if a leader is going through a difficult time, they might share their experience with the team in a way that is honest and constructive. This not only humanizes the leader but also encourages team members to support one another and create a culture of empathy within the organization.

4. **Create Opportunities for Team Connection**: Empathy thrives in environments where team members feel connected to one another. Leaders can foster empathy by creating opportunities for team members to bond and build relationships. This might include team-building activities, social events, or informal check-ins where team members can share their experiences and get to know each other on a personal level.

   Additionally, leaders can encourage team members to practice empathy by creating a culture of peer support. This involves empowering team members to look out for one another, offer help when needed, and collaborate in a way that is compassionate and respectful.

5. **Engage in Regular Reflection and Feedback**: Developing empathy is an ongoing process, and leaders should regularly reflect on their empathetic behavior and seek feedback from others. By asking for input from team members, colleagues, or mentors, leaders can gain valuable insights into how their empathy is perceived and identify areas for improvement.

   Leaders can also engage in **self-reflection** by keeping a journal where they document their interactions with team members, noting how they responded to emotional cues and what they might do differently in the future. This practice of reflection helps leaders become more intentional in their empathetic leadership and ensures that they are continuously growing in this area.

Establishing an Empathy Culture in the Company

Empathetic leadership is not just about individual leaders practicing empathy; it's about creating a culture of empathy that permeates the entire organization. When empathy is embedded in the organizational culture, it becomes a shared value that guides how employees interact with one another and how the organization approaches its goals.

1. **Establish Core Values That Reflect Empathy**: Leaders can start by embedding empathy into the organization's core values. This involves clearly articulating that empathy, compassion, and respect are central to the organization's mission and that

these values should guide all interactions, both internally and externally.
2. **Provide Empathy Training**: Organizations can offer training programs that focus on developing empathy and emotional intelligence. These programs might include workshops, seminars, or coaching sessions that help employees at all levels build empathy skills, such as active listening, emotional regulation, and conflict resolution.
3. **Encourage Empathetic Leadership at All Levels**: Empathy should not be limited to senior leadership; it should be encouraged at all levels of the organization. By empowering managers, team leaders, and employees to practice empathy in their roles, organizations can create a more supportive and cohesive work environment.
4. **Recognize and Reward Empathy**: To reinforce the importance of empathy, organizations can implement recognition programs that reward employees who demonstrate exceptional empathy and compassion in their interactions with others. This helps to signal that empathy is valued and encourages employees to continue practicing empathetic behavior.

Empathy is a powerful leadership skill that can be developed and cultivated through self-awareness, emotional regulation, active listening, and a commitment to understanding others. By overcoming barriers to empathy and practicing empathetic leadership in everyday interactions, leaders can create a positive, supportive, and productive work environment.

CHAPTER FOUR

THE IMPACT OF EMPATHY ON ORGANIZATIONAL SUCCESS

Empathy is more than just a "nice-to-have" quality in leadership—it is a critical component of organizational success. In today's increasingly complex and competitive business environment, companies that prioritize empathy in their leadership and culture experience tangible benefits such as higher employee engagement, greater innovation, improved customer relationships, and stronger financial performance. In this chapter, we will explore the many ways in which empathy drives organizational success, backed by research and real-world examples. We will also look at case studies of leaders who have transformed their teams and companies by making empathy a core value in their leadership approach.

The Link Between Empathy and Employee Engagement

Worker engagement is the passionate commitment that workers ought to their organization and its objectives. Engaged employees are more likely to go above and beyond in their roles, contribute creative ideas, and remain loyal to the organization. Numerous studies have shown that empathetic leadership is strongly linked to higher levels of employee engagement.

1. **Fostering a Sense of Belonging**: Empathetic leaders create an environment where employees feel valued, understood, and supported. This sense of belonging is a key driver of employee

engagement. When employees believe that their leaders genuinely care about their well-being and are invested in their success, they are more likely to feel connected to the organization and motivated to contribute.

Research has shown that employees who feel a sense of belonging at work are significantly more engaged and productive. According to a study by the Harvard Business Review, 94% of employees who reported feeling cared for by their leaders said they were engaged at work, compared to just 38% of employees who did not feel cared for. This demonstrates the powerful impact that empathy can have on creating a more engaged and motivated workforce.

2. **Building Trust and Psychological Safety**: Empathy plays a critical role in building trust between leaders and their teams. Trust is a foundational element of employee engagement, as it allows employees to feel safe in taking risks, sharing ideas, and voicing concerns. Empathetic leaders foster trust by demonstrating that they understand and care about their employees' perspectives, and by responding to their needs with compassion and support.

In organizations with high levels of trust, employees are more likely to experience **psychological safety**—the belief that they can express themselves without fear of negative consequences. Psychological safety is essential for employee engagement because it encourages open communication, collaboration, and creativity. When employees feel safe to be themselves and share their thoughts freely, they are more likely to be fully engaged in their work.

3. **Reducing Turnover and Burnout**: Empathetic leadership is also linked to lower employee turnover and reduced burnout. In organizations where leaders prioritize empathy, employees are less likely to experience chronic stress, emotional exhaustion, and disengagement—key factors that contribute to burnout. By recognizing and addressing the emotional needs of their employees, empathetic leaders help to create a healthier work environment where employees can thrive.

High employee turnover is costly for organizations in terms of lost productivity, recruitment, and training. However, organizations that invest in empathetic leadership are more likely to retain their top talent. A study by the Society for Human Resource Management (SHRM) found that 91% of employees who felt their leaders were empathetic were less likely to leave their jobs, compared to only 36% of employees who did not feel their leaders were empathetic. This illustrates how empathy not only enhances employee engagement but also helps organizations retain their valuable workforce.

Empathy as a Driver of Innovation

Advancement is the soul of organizational development and competitiveness. Organizations that consistently innovate are better equipped to adapt to changing market conditions, meet evolving customer needs, and stay ahead of the competition. Empathy is a key driver of innovation because it fosters a culture of creativity, collaboration, and open-mindedness.

1. **Understanding Customer Needs**: Empathy is essential for innovation because it allows leaders and teams to deeply understand the needs, desires, and pain points of their customers. By putting themselves in their customers' shoes, empathetic leaders can identify opportunities for new products, services, or improvements that directly address customer needs.

    Design thinking, a popular framework for innovation, places empathy at the center of the innovation process. The first step in design thinking is to **empathize** with the customer—gaining a deep understanding of their experiences, challenges, and motivations. By approaching innovation with empathy, organizations are more likely to develop solutions that resonate with their customers and provide real value.

    A well-known example of empathy-driven innovation is the success of apple under the leadership of Steve Jobs. While Jobs was not always viewed as an empathetic leader in his management style, his ability to empathize with customers' desires for intuitive, beautifully designed technology was key to Apple's innovation success. Jobs' emphasis on understanding how people interact with technology led to the development of groundbreaking products like the iPhone, which revolutionized the smartphone industry by prioritizing user experience.

2. **Fostering a Collaborative Environment**: Empathy also drives innovation by creating a collaborative environment where team members feel comfortable sharing ideas, giving feedback, and working together to solve problems. In organizations where leaders demonstrate empathy, employees are more likely to feel valued and respected, which encourages them to contribute their unique perspectives and insights.

    Collaboration is essential for innovation because it allows diverse ideas to come together, leading to more creative and well-rounded solutions. Empathetic leaders facilitate collaboration by actively listening to their team members, validating their ideas, and encouraging open communication. When employees feel that their voices are heard and respected, they are more likely to contribute innovative ideas that can drive the organization forward.

3. **Encouraging Risk-Taking and Experimentation**: Innovation often involves taking risks and trying new approaches, which can be daunting for employees if they fear failure or negative consequences. Empathetic leaders create

an environment where employees feel safe to experiment and take risks without the fear of being punished for failure.

Empathy allows leaders to understand the emotional challenges that come with risk-taking and to provide the support and encouragement that employees need to step out of their comfort zones. By fostering a culture where mistakes are seen as learning opportunities rather than failures, empathetic leaders empower their teams to innovate more freely and push the boundaries of what is possible.

Enhancing Customer Relationships Through Empathy

Empathy is not only important for internal organizational dynamics; it is also a critical factor in building strong, lasting relationships with customers. In today's customer-centric business landscape, organizations that demonstrate empathy in their interactions with customers are more likely to earn their trust, loyalty, and repeat business.

1. **Personalized Customer Experiences**: Empathetic organizations prioritize understanding the individual needs and preferences of their customers, allowing them to provide personalized experiences that resonate on a deeper level. By taking the time to listen to their customers and understand their unique challenges, organizations can tailor their products, services, and

communication to meet those needs more effectively.

A prime example of empathy-driven customer service is Zappos, the online shoe and clothing retailer known for its exceptional customer service. Zappos' leadership encourages employees to go above and beyond to understand and meet the needs of customers, even if it means deviating from standard procedures. This customer-first approach has helped Zappos build a loyal customer base and differentiate itself in a competitive market.

2. **Resolving Customer Complaints with Compassion**: Empathy is especially important in handling customer complaints and resolving issues. When clients experience issues, they need to feel listened and caught on. Empathetic leaders and customer service teams are better equipped to de-escalate conflicts and find solutions that satisfy the customer.

By demonstrating empathy in customer interactions, organizations can turn potentially negative experiences into opportunities to build trust and loyalty. For example, when a customer feels that their concerns have been genuinely acknowledged and addressed, they are more likely to forgive the mistake and continue doing business with the company.

3. **Building Long-Term Loyalty**: Empathy plays a central role in building long-term customer loyalty.

Customers are more likely to remain loyal to a brand or company that they believe understands and values them. This emotional connection is a powerful differentiator in a crowded marketplace, where customers have many options to choose from.

Companies that prioritize empathy in their customer relationships are more likely to enjoy higher levels of customer retention and repeat business. A study by PwC found that 82% of customers want more human interaction in their customer experiences, and 59% said they would stop doing business with a company after just a few bad experiences. This highlights the importance of empathy in creating positive, meaningful customer interactions that foster loyalty.

Empathy and Organizational Performance

In addition to its impact on employee engagement, innovation, and customer relationships, empathy also has a direct influence on an organization's overall performance and financial success. While empathy may be seen as a "soft" skill, research shows that it has a measurable impact on key business outcomes.

1. **Higher Productivity and Efficiency**: Empathetic leadership creates a work environment where employees feel motivated, supported, and engaged. As a result, employees are more likely to perform at their best, leading to higher levels of productivity and efficiency. When employees

believe that their leaders care about their well-being and are invested in their success, they are more likely to take ownership of their work and contribute to the organization's goals.

A study by the consulting firm Catalyst found that employees who worked for empathetic leaders were more likely to report higher levels of productivity and satisfaction. In fact, 61% of employees who felt their leaders were empathetic said they were more likely to stay with their current employer, and 76% reported feeling more engaged at work.

2. **Improved Employee Retention and Recruitment**: Organizations with empathetic leadership are more likely to retain their top talent and attract high-quality candidates. In today's competitive job market, employees are increasingly seeking workplaces where they feel valued, respected, and supported. Empathetic organizations have a clear advantage in recruiting and retaining talent, as they are able to offer a positive, supportive work environment that appeals to job seekers.
3. **Stronger Financial Performance**: Ultimately, organizations that prioritize empathy in their leadership and culture tend to experience stronger financial performance. A study by the business consulting firm Development Dimensions International (DDI) found that companies with high levels of empathy in their leadership outperform their competitors in terms of revenue growth and profitability. The study revealed that empathetic

organizations generated 50% more revenue than those with low levels of empathy, highlighting the clear connection between empathy and business success.

Empathy is not just a moral imperative for leaders—it is a strategic advantage that drives organizational success. From enhancing employee engagement and fostering innovation to improving customer relationships and driving financial performance, empathy has a profound impact on all aspects of an organization. By making empathy a core value in their leadership approach, leaders can create a positive, supportive, and high-performing work environment where teams and companies can thrive.

CHAPTER FIVE

CHALLENGES OF PRACTICING EMPATHY IN LEADERSHIP

Empathy is a powerful leadership tool, but practicing empathy effectively in the workplace comes with its own set of challenges. While the benefits of empathetic leadership are well-documented, there are many obstacles that leaders must overcome to implement empathy in a meaningful and sustainable way. Leaders may face resistance from traditional leadership norms, cultural differences, emotional exhaustion, and the complexity of balancing empathy with the need to make difficult business decisions. In this chapter, we will explore these challenges in detail and provide strategies for overcoming them, so leaders can continue to lead with empathy while maintaining organizational efficiency and effectiveness.

The Pressure to Maintain Traditional Leadership Norms

1. Balancing Empathy and Authority

One of the first challenges empathetic leaders encounter is the pressure to conform to traditional leadership norms that prioritize authority, toughness, and detachment over compassion. In many corporate cultures, there is still an ingrained belief that leaders should remain emotionally distant and prioritize business results over personal relationships. This expectation creates a tension between demonstrating empathy and maintaining authority.

Leaders often worry that showing too much empathy might make them appear weak or compromise their ability to enforce discipline and hold employees accountable. Balancing empathy with the need for authority is a delicate challenge, as leaders must find a way to show compassion without undermining their role as decision-makers.

However, empathy does not have to come at the expense of authority. In fact, empathetic leaders can enhance their authority by demonstrating that they understand their team members' needs and concerns while still making objective, fair decisions. To strike this balance, leaders can:

- **Set clear boundaries**: While practicing empathy, leaders must establish boundaries that clarify their role and the organization's goals. This means communicating expectations clearly and explaining how empathetic leadership aligns with the pursuit of business objectives.
- **Lead with consistency**: Leaders who are both empathetic and authoritative are consistent in their actions. They hold employees accountable while addressing their challenges compassionately. For example, if an employee is struggling with personal issues that affect their performance, an empathetic leader can offer support while also making it clear that performance expectations remain in place.
- **Frame empathy as a strength**: Leaders can redefine the narrative around empathy by presenting it as a strength, rather than a weakness. When leaders show empathy, they can enhance team cohesion and improve problem-

solving, which ultimately supports organizational goals. By viewing empathy as a strategic tool, leaders can integrate it into their leadership style without feeling pressured to conform to outdated norms.

2. **Resistance to Change within the Organization**

Another significant challenge in practicing empathetic leadership is resistance to change from within the organization. In companies that have historically emphasized a more hierarchical or results-driven leadership style, there may be skepticism or resistance to a shift toward empathy.

Some employees and colleagues might question the effectiveness of empathy-driven leadership, viewing it as overly emotional or unproductive. This resistance can come from all levels of the organization, from frontline employees to senior executives. Leaders must navigate this pushback and find ways to demonstrate that empathy leads to better outcomes without undermining their credibility.

Strategies to overcome resistance to change include:

- **Communicating the benefits of empathy**: Leaders should make a compelling case for why empathetic leadership is essential for the organization's success. This can be achieved by highlighting research that shows the positive impact of empathy on employee engagement, innovation, and customer satisfaction, and by

sharing success stories of companies that have embraced empathetic leadership with great results.
- **Leading by example**: Leaders who model empathetic behavior can inspire others to follow suit. By consistently demonstrating empathy in their interactions with employees, leaders can gradually shift the culture and show that empathy is not only effective but also integral to achieving business goals.
- **Starting small**: Leaders can introduce empathy into the organization incrementally. For example, they might begin by incorporating empathy into team meetings, one-on-one interactions, or performance reviews. As employees start to see the benefits of empathy in these smaller settings, they may be more open to embracing it on a larger scale.

Cultural and Generational Differences in Empathy

In today's global and diverse workplace, leaders must also navigate cultural and generational differences that can affect how empathy is expressed and understood. Empathy is not a one-size-fits-all concept; what is considered empathetic behavior in one culture or generation might not be perceived the same way in another. Leaders who want to practice empathy effectively must be aware of these differences and adapt their approach accordingly.

1. Cultural Differences in Empathy

Different cultures have different expectations around emotional expression, communication styles, and leadership. For example, in some cultures, expressing vulnerability or discussing personal issues may be seen as inappropriate in the workplace, while in others, it might be encouraged as a way to build trust and rapport.

Leaders working in a multicultural environment must be mindful of these cultural differences and ensure that their empathetic behavior is culturally sensitive. This might involve adjusting communication styles, being aware of non-verbal cues, and understanding the cultural context of their team members.

To navigate cultural differences in empathy, leaders can:

- **Develop cultural competence**: Leaders should invest time in learning about the cultures represented on their teams. This includes understanding cultural norms around emotional expression, leadership, and communication. Leaders can also seek guidance from cultural experts or engage in diversity and inclusion training to enhance their understanding.
- **Ask questions and listen**: Empathy involves listening to others and seeking to understand their experiences. Leaders can show empathy by asking questions about how cultural differences might impact their team members' expectations and preferences. This helps leaders tailor their empathetic approach to each individual, rather than applying a one-size-fits-all strategy.
- **Create a culture of openness**: Leaders can foster an environment where cultural differences are acknowledged and celebrated. By encouraging open dialogue about cultural expectations, leaders

can create a workplace where team members feel comfortable expressing their needs and preferences, leading to greater understanding and empathy.

2. Generational Differences in Empathy

Generational differences in the workplace can also pose challenges for empathetic leadership. With multiple generations working side by side, leaders must navigate varying expectations around communication, work-life balance, and leadership styles. For example, younger generations, such as Millennials and Generation Z, may place a greater emphasis on work-life balance and mental health, while older generations might prioritize hard work and resilience.

Leaders must recognize these generational differences and practice empathy by understanding the unique perspectives and needs of each group. This can be achieved by:

- **Adapting communication styles**: Different generations may have different preferences for how they receive and give feedback. For example, younger employees might appreciate more frequent, informal check-ins, while older employees may prefer formal performance reviews. Leaders should be flexible in their communication approach to meet the needs of each generation.
- **Supporting diverse work-life balance needs**: Leaders can demonstrate empathy by offering flexible work arrangements that cater to different generational preferences. For instance, younger

employees might value remote work options or flexible hours, while older employees might appreciate stability and consistency in their schedules.
- **Fostering intergenerational collaboration**: Leaders can promote empathy across generations by encouraging collaboration and knowledge sharing between team members of different age groups. This helps to bridge generational gaps and fosters mutual understanding and respect.

Emotional Exhaustion and Compassion Fatigue

One of the risks of practicing empathy in leadership is the potential for emotional exhaustion and compassion fatigue. Leaders who are highly empathetic may find themselves emotionally drained by the constant demands of caring for their team members, particularly in high-stress or crisis situations. Compassion fatigue occurs when leaders become overwhelmed by the emotional burden of empathizing with others, leading to burnout and a decline in their ability to lead effectively.

To prevent emotional exhaustion and compassion fatigue, leaders must prioritize their own well-being and set healthy boundaries. Strategies for managing emotional fatigue include:

1. **Practicing Self-Compassion**

Leaders who are empathetic toward others must also extend that empathy to themselves. Practicing self-compassion involves recognizing that leadership is challenging, and it is okay to feel overwhelmed at times.

Leaders can show themselves empathy by acknowledging their emotions, allowing themselves time to rest, and seeking support when needed.

2. **Setting Boundaries**

Empathetic leaders must establish clear boundaries to protect their emotional well-being. This might involve setting limits on how much time and energy they devote to supporting others, delegating tasks to prevent overwhelm, and taking time for self-care. Leaders should also be mindful of not taking on their team members' emotional burdens as their own.

3. **Seeking Support and Supervision**

Leaders who regularly engage in empathetic leadership can benefit from seeking support from peers, mentors, or coaches. Talking through challenges with others who understand the demands of leadership can help alleviate emotional exhaustion and provide valuable perspective. Additionally, supervision or coaching can offer guidance on how to navigate emotionally charged situations without becoming overwhelmed.

4. **Engaging in Stress-Relief Practices**

Leaders should incorporate stress-relief practices into their routine to manage the emotional demands of empathetic leadership. This might include mindfulness meditation, exercise, journaling, or spending time in nature. By making time for activities that promote relaxation and mental well-being, leaders can recharge and maintain their emotional resilience.

Balancing Empathy with Tough Decision-Making

Another challenge empathetic leaders face is balancing empathy with the need to make tough business decisions. While empathy is essential for building strong relationships and fostering a positive work environment, leaders must also make difficult decisions that may not always align with the immediate desires or emotions of their team members.

For example, leaders may need to implement layoffs, cut budgets, or restructure teams to ensure the organization's long-term success. These decisions can create emotional distress for employees, and leaders must find a way to navigate these situations with empathy while still making objective, business-driven choices.

To balance empathy with tough decision-making, leaders can:

1. **Communicate Transparently**

When making difficult decisions, empathetic leaders prioritize transparent communication. This means being open and honest about the reasons behind the decision, while also acknowledging the emotional impact it may have on employees. Leaders who communicate with empathy can help employees understand the context of the decision and reduce feelings of confusion or resentment.

2. **Show Compassion in Execution**

Even when making tough decisions, leaders can show compassion in how they execute those decisions. For example, during layoffs, leaders can offer support to affected employees by providing severance packages, career counseling, or assistance in finding new job opportunities. Showing compassion during difficult times helps maintain trust and respect between leaders and employees.

3. **Provide Opportunities for Feedback**

Leaders can balance empathy with tough decision-making by creating opportunities for employees to provide feedback and voice their concerns. While the decision may not change, giving employees a chance to express their emotions and be heard can help alleviate some of the distress. Leaders can then use this feedback to improve how they handle similar situations in the future.

Practicing empathy in leadership is not without its challenges, but the rewards are well worth the effort. By navigating the pressures of traditional leadership norms, understanding cultural and generational differences, managing emotional exhaustion, and balancing empathy with tough decision-making, leaders can create a more compassionate, engaged, and successful workplace.

CHAPTER SIX

TOOLS AND TECHNIQUES FOR DEVELOPING EMPATHY IN LEADERSHIP

In the modern workplace, empathy is a vital skill that allows leaders to connect with their teams, foster a positive work environment, and drive organizational success. However, empathy is not always an innate trait—it is a skill that can be developed and strengthened with practice and intentionality. For leaders who want to enhance their empathetic abilities, there are a variety of tools, techniques, and practices that can help them cultivate empathy in their daily interactions and leadership approach.

This chapter will explore practical strategies for developing empathy, including active listening, emotional intelligence, mindfulness practices, perspective-taking exercises, and building deeper relationships with team members. By incorporating these tools into their leadership style, leaders can become more attuned to the needs and emotions of their teams, leading to stronger communication, increased trust, and improved performance.

The Importance of Active Listening

1. **Understanding Active Listening**

One of the most important tools for developing empathy is active listening. Active listening involves fully engaging with another person's words, emotions, and nonverbal cues, rather than simply waiting for your turn to speak. It requires leaders to be present in the conversation and to genuinely seek to understand the other person's perspective.

Active listening goes beyond hearing the words someone is saying; it involves understanding the meaning behind those words, as well as the emotions driving them. This deeper level of listening allows leaders to connect with their team members on a more profound level and respond in ways that show they truly understand their concerns and feelings.

2. **Techniques for Improving Active Listening**

Leaders can strengthen their active listening skills through practice and intentionality. Some key techniques for improving active listening include:

- **Maintaining eye contact**: Eye contact signals that you are paying attention and are fully present in the conversation. It helps to build trust and demonstrates your genuine interest in what the other person is saying.
- **Avoiding distractions**: When listening to someone, it's essential to eliminate distractions that could take your focus away from the conversation. This includes putting away your phone, avoiding multitasking, and giving the speaker your full attention.
- **Reflecting back key points**: After the other person has spoken, it can be helpful to summarize or paraphrase what they've said to ensure that you've understood their message. This not only shows that you are listening but also gives the

speaker the opportunity to clarify any misunderstandings.
- **Asking open-ended questions**: Empathetic leaders ask questions that encourage the speaker to share more about their thoughts and feelings. Open-ended questions, such as "Can you tell me more about that?" or "How did that situation make you feel?" help to deepen the conversation and demonstrate genuine curiosity about the other person's perspective.
- **Responding with empathy**: After listening to someone's concerns, it's important to respond in a way that acknowledges their emotions and validates their experiences. Phrases like "I understand why you're feeling that way" or "That sounds really challenging" show that you are empathetic to their situation.

3. **The Benefits of Active Listening in Leadership**

Active listening has numerous benefits for leaders and their teams. When leaders practice active listening, they create an environment where team members feel heard, valued, and understood. This fosters a sense of trust and psychological safety, which encourages employees to speak up, share ideas, and collaborate more effectively.

Additionally, active listening allows leaders to identify potential issues or challenges before they escalate. By paying close attention to the concerns and emotions of their team members, leaders can address problems proactively and find solutions that meet the needs of both the individual and the organization.

Enhancing Emotional Intelligence

1. What is Emotional Intelligence?

Emotional intelligence (EQ) is the ability to recognize, understand, and manage your own emotions, as well as the emotions of others. It plays a critical role in empathetic leadership because it enables leaders to navigate complex emotional dynamics, respond appropriately to different situations, and build strong relationships with their teams.

There are five key components of passionate insights:

- **Self-awareness**: The ability to recognize and understand your own emotions, as well as how they impact your thoughts, behaviors, and interactions with others.
- **Self-regulation**: The ability to manage and control your emotions, particularly in stressful or challenging situations, so that you can respond calmly and effectively.
- **Motivation**: A strong sense of purpose and drive that helps you stay focused on your goals and overcome obstacles.
- **Empathy**: The ability to understand and share the feelings of others, which allows you to connect with people on a deeper level.
- **Social skills**: The ability to build and maintain positive relationships, communicate effectively, and navigate social situations with ease.

2. **Developing Emotional Intelligence**

Emotional intelligence can be developed and strengthened over time through self-reflection, feedback, and practice. Some strategies for enhancing emotional intelligence include:

- **Practicing mindfulness**: Mindfulness involves paying attention to the present moment and observing your thoughts, feelings, and physical sensations without judgment. By practicing mindfulness regularly, leaders can become more attuned to their own emotions and learn to manage them in a healthier way.
- **Seeking feedback from others**: One of the most effective ways to improve emotional intelligence is to seek feedback from others, particularly in areas where you may have blind spots. Colleagues, mentors, or coaches can provide valuable insights into how you are perceived by others and help you identify areas for growth.
- **Reflecting on emotional experiences**: After emotionally charged situations, take time to reflect on how you handled your emotions and how your emotions impacted your decisions and interactions. Consider what you could do differently next time to manage your emotions more effectively.
- **Empathy practice**: Emotional intelligence can be enhanced by actively practicing empathy. This involves putting yourself in the shoes of others, imagining how they might feel in a particular

situation, and considering their perspective before reacting or making decisions.

3. **The Role of Emotional Intelligence in Leadership**

The Part of Enthusiastic Insights in Authority Pioneers with tall passionate insights are superior prepared to handle the enthusiastic complexities of authority . They can manage their own stress and emotions, respond to challenges with composure, and navigate difficult conversations with empathy and understanding. This emotional resilience allows them to remain effective even in high-pressure situations, which in turn builds trust and confidence within their teams.

Moreover, emotionally intelligent leaders are able to read the emotions of others and respond in ways that make their team members feel supported, valued, and understood. This leads to stronger relationships, increased collaboration, and a more positive work environment overall.

Mindfulness Practices for Empathy

1. **The Connection Between Mindfulness and Empathy**

Mindfulness is the practice of bringing focused attention to the present moment and observing one's thoughts, emotions, and sensations without judgment. Mindfulness and empathy are closely connected, as mindfulness helps leaders become more aware of their own emotions and the emotions of others. By practicing mindfulness, leaders can develop greater emotional regulation, focus, and presence, which are all essential for practicing empathy effectively.

Mindful leaders are more attuned to their team members' needs and can respond thoughtfully rather than reacting impulsively. They are also more present in their interactions, which allows them to listen deeply and understand the emotions behind their team members' words.

2. **Mindfulness Techniques for Leaders**

There are several mindfulness practices that leaders can incorporate into their daily routines to enhance their empathetic abilities:

- **Mindful breathing**: This involves focusing on the breath as a way to center the mind and bring attention to the present moment. Mindful breathing can be practiced for a few minutes at the beginning of the day, before important meetings, or whenever a leader feels overwhelmed or stressed.
- **Body scan meditation**: In a body scan meditation, leaders bring awareness to different parts of their body, noticing any areas of tension or discomfort. This practice helps leaders become more attuned to their physical sensations, which can provide insight into their emotional state.
- **Loving-kindness meditation**: Loving-kindness meditation involves sending feelings of compassion and goodwill to oneself and others. Leaders can use this practice to cultivate empathy by focusing

on specific team members or colleagues, wishing them happiness, health, and success.
- **Mindful listening**: During conversations, leaders can practice mindful listening by giving their full attention to the speaker, without interrupting or formulating a response in their mind. This helps leaders become more present in their interactions and fosters deeper understanding and connection.

3. The Benefits of Mindfulness for Leadership

Pioneers who hone mindfulness encounter various benefits, counting decreased stretch, moved forward enthusiastic control, and upgraded center. Mindfulness also supports empathetic leadership by helping leaders stay present in their interactions, listen more deeply, and respond thoughtfully to their team members' needs.

Perspective-Taking Exercises

1. What is Perspective-Taking?

Perspective-taking is the capacity to get it and consider another person's point of see. It goes beyond empathy by actively imagining what it would be like to walk in someone else's shoes, experiencing the world as they do. This skill is particularly important for leaders, as it allows them to make more informed and empathetic decisions that take into account the diverse perspectives of their team members.

2. Exercises for Improving Perspective-Taking

Leaders can enhance their perspective-taking abilities through specific exercises and practices, such as:

- **Role-playing**: In role-playing exercises, leaders can take on the role of a team member, client, or colleague to better understand their point of view. This helps leaders gain insight into the challenges and experiences of others, which can inform their decision-making.
- **Journaling from another person's perspective**: Leaders can strengthen their perspective-taking by journaling from the point of view of someone else. For example, they might write about a particular situation from the perspective of an employee, considering how that person might feel and what they might need from leadership.
- **Empathy mapping**: Empathy mapping is a visual tool that helps leaders understand the emotions, thoughts, and needs of others. By creating an empathy map for a team member or stakeholder, leaders can identify key areas where they can provide support or make more empathetic decisions.

3. **The Role of Perspective-Taking in Leadership**

Perspective-taking allows leaders to make more inclusive and empathetic decisions by considering the diverse needs and viewpoints of their team members. It also helps leaders navigate conflicts and challenges with greater understanding, as they are able to see the situation from multiple angles. Ultimately, perspective-taking enhances leaders' ability to connect with their teams and create a more supportive, collaborative work environment.

Building Deeper Relationships with Team Members

1. The Importance of Relationship Building in Leadership

Empathy in leadership is most effective when it is built on a foundation of strong relationships. Leaders who invest time in getting to know their team members on a personal level are better able to understand their unique needs, motivations, and challenges. This deeper understanding fosters trust and loyalty, which in turn leads to greater collaboration and team cohesion.

2. Strategies for Building Stronger Relationships

Leaders can build deeper relationships with their team members by:

- **Scheduling regular one-on-one meetings**: One-on-one meetings provide an opportunity for leaders to connect with their team members individually and discuss their goals, challenges, and well-being. These meetings should focus on building rapport and understanding the team member's needs, rather than just addressing work-related tasks.
- **Showing genuine interest in team members' lives**: Leaders can build stronger relationships by showing a genuine interest in their team members' personal lives, hobbies, and interests. This helps to humanize the leader and creates a sense of connection beyond the workplace.

- **Celebrating successes and supporting challenges**: Empathetic leaders celebrate their team members' successes and provide support during difficult times. Whether it's offering praise for a job well done or providing resources during a personal challenge, these actions demonstrate that the leader cares about the well-being of their team members.

3. **The Impact of Strong Relationships on Team Performance**

When leaders build strong, empathetic relationships with their team members, it leads to greater trust, collaboration, and engagement. Team members are more likely to feel supported, valued, and motivated to contribute to the organization's success. This, in turn, leads to improved performance, innovation, and overall job satisfaction.

Developing empathy in leadership is a continuous process that requires intentional practice and self-reflection. By incorporating tools such as active listening, emotional intelligence, mindfulness, perspective-taking, and relationship-building into their leadership approach, leaders can cultivate deeper connections with their teams and create a more compassionate, effective work environment.

CHAPTER SEVEN

CASE STUDIES OF EMPATHETIC LEADERSHIP IN ACTION

As empathy becomes an increasingly valued trait in the workplace, more leaders are realizing the profound impact it can have on organizational culture, team performance, and individual well-being. However, empathy is not just a theoretical concept; it has been successfully implemented by many leaders across industries, leading to tangible improvements in productivity, innovation, and employee satisfaction.

This chapter will explore a series of case studies that showcase empathetic leadership in action. These examples will illustrate how leaders have used empathy to navigate challenges, foster collaboration, and create a more supportive and engaged workforce. By examining these real-world examples, readers will gain a deeper understanding of how empathy can be applied in various leadership contexts, as well as the outcomes it can generate.

Case Study 1: Empathy in Crisis Management – The Example of Microsoft

One of the most notable examples of empathetic leadership comes from Satya Nadella, the CEO of Microsoft. Nadella's approach to leadership is deeply rooted in empathy, which has had a transformative effect on the company's culture and performance.

Background: When Nadella became CEO of Microsoft in 2014, the company was facing significant challenges, including declining innovation, internal competition, and a rigid, hierarchical culture. Many employees felt disconnected from the company's mission, and morale was low. Nadella recognized that in order to revitalize Microsoft, he needed to foster a more inclusive, collaborative, and empathetic culture.

Empathy in Action: One of Nadella's first actions as CEO was to shift Microsoft's focus from a "know-it-all" culture to a "learn-it-all" culture. This meant encouraging curiosity, collaboration, and open communication, rather than competition and rigid expertise. Nadella emphasized the importance of understanding the needs of customers, employees, and partners, and he led by example by listening to others' perspectives and showing vulnerability in his own leadership.

Nadella also prioritized diversity and inclusion, recognizing that a more empathetic, inclusive workplace would lead to better innovation and problem-solving. Under his leadership, Microsoft implemented initiatives to support underrepresented groups, foster a culture of belonging, and promote empathy at all levels of the organization.

Outcome: Nadella's empathetic leadership has been widely credited with transforming Microsoft's culture and driving its resurgence as a leading tech company. The company's market value has more than tripled since Nadella took over, and employee engagement and satisfaction have significantly improved. Microsoft has also been recognized for its commitment to diversity and inclusion, with Nadella's empathetic leadership serving as a model for other organizations.

Case Study 2: Empathy in Organizational Change – Starbucks' Response to Crisis

In 2018, Starbucks faced a public relations crisis when two Black men were arrested at one of the company's Philadelphia locations while waiting for a friend. The incident sparked widespread outrage and raised concerns about racial bias within the company.

Background: Starbucks, a global coffeehouse chain known for its customer-centric approach, found itself at the center of a national conversation about racial profiling and discrimination. The company's leadership, under CEO Kevin Johnson, recognized that this crisis required more than a standard PR response. It demanded a genuine display of empathy, both toward the individuals affected and the broader public.

Empathy in Action: Johnson immediately took responsibility for the incident, publicly apologizing to the two men and acknowledging the need for change within the company. He flew to Philadelphia to meet with the men personally, demonstrating empathy through direct engagement.

In addition to the personal apology, Johnson took swift and meaningful action to address the underlying issues. Starbucks closed more than 8,000 stores across the United States for a day of racial bias training, a bold move that signaled the company's commitment to fostering a more inclusive and empathetic culture. The training, which was designed in collaboration with civil rights experts, focused on understanding unconscious bias and building empathy among employees.

Johnson also implemented structural changes to prevent similar incidents in the future. This included revising company policies, such as allowing people to use Starbucks' restrooms and seating areas without making a purchase, to create a more welcoming environment for all customers.

Outcome: While Starbucks faced significant criticism in the immediate aftermath of the incident, Johnson's empathetic response helped to restore the company's reputation and rebuild trust with both customers and employees. The racial bias training initiative was seen as a positive step toward addressing systemic issues within the company, and Starbucks continues to be viewed as a leader in corporate social responsibility. The incident also highlighted the importance of empathy in navigating crises and making meaningful organizational changes.

Case Study 3: Empathy in Employee Well-being – The Example of Zoom

As the COVID-19 pandemic forced millions of people to work remotely, Zoom Video Communications became an essential tool for maintaining communication and collaboration. However, the company itself faced immense pressure to scale rapidly while ensuring the well-being of its employees.

Background: Zoom's popularity skyrocketed during the pandemic, leading to a 30-fold increase in users within just a few months. While this rapid growth was a positive sign for the company's business, it also placed immense stress on its employees, many of whom were working long hours to support the increased demand for Zoom's services. Zoom's leadership, under CEO Eric Yuan, recognized the importance of empathy in addressing the challenges faced by its workforce during this unprecedented time.

Empathy in Action: Yuan prioritized employee well-being by implementing several initiatives aimed at reducing stress and supporting mental health. Zoom provided employees with additional time off, flexible work schedules, and access to mental health resources, including counseling and wellness programs. Yuan also communicated regularly with employees, offering transparent updates about the company's response to the pandemic and encouraging open dialogue about the challenges they were facing.

In addition to supporting its own employees, Zoom extended its empathetic approach to its customers and the broader community. Yuan made the company's video conferencing services available for free to schools, healthcare providers, and other organizations that were particularly impacted by the pandemic. This decision was driven by Yuan's belief that empathy should extend beyond the workplace and into the broader society.

Outcome: Zoom's empathetic leadership during the pandemic not only helped to support its employees' well-being but also contributed to the company's continued success. The company's stock price soared, and it became one of the most recognized and trusted brands during the pandemic. Moreover, Zoom's empathetic response to the challenges of the pandemic earned it a positive reputation for corporate social responsibility and employee care.

Case Study 4: Empathy in Innovation – The Approach of IDEO

IDEO, a global design and consulting firm, is known for its human-centered approach to innovation, which places empathy at the core of its design process. The company's leadership has cultivated a culture of empathy that drives its creative problem-solving and product development.

Background: IDEO's design philosophy is built on the belief that innovation starts with empathy—understanding the needs, desires, and emotions of the people for whom products and services are designed. This empathetic approach not only leads to more effective solutions but also fosters a collaborative, inclusive work environment.

Empathy in Action: At IDEO, empathy is embedded in every stage of the design process. The company uses techniques such as ethnographic research, interviews, and observation to deeply understand the experiences and pain points of end users. IDEO designers frequently immerse themselves in the environments of their clients and customers to gain firsthand insight into their needs.

IDEO's empathetic approach to leadership extends beyond its design process. The company fosters a collaborative, inclusive culture in which employees are encouraged to share their ideas and perspectives. Leadership promotes open communication, active listening, and a sense of psychological safety, allowing employees to feel comfortable taking creative risks.

Outcome: IDEO's empathetic approach has resulted in a number of groundbreaking innovations, from the design of the first Apple mouse to the development of innovative healthcare solutions. The company's success demonstrates how empathy can drive innovation by ensuring that products and services are designed with the end user's needs and emotions in mind. Additionally, IDEO's empathetic leadership has contributed to a strong, collaborative organizational culture that attracts top talent and fosters creativity.

Case Study 5: Empathy in Employee Development – The Leadership of Patagonia

Patagonia, the outdoor apparel company, has long been recognized for its commitment to environmental sustainability and social responsibility. Under the leadership of its founder, Yvon Chouinard, Patagonia has also become a model for empathetic leadership, particularly in its approach to employee development and well-being.

Background: Patagonia's leadership philosophy is rooted in the belief that businesses should prioritize the well-being of their employees and the environment over short-term profits. This empathetic approach has shaped the company's culture, policies, and practices, creating a supportive environment in which employees are encouraged to thrive both personally and professionally.

Empathy in Action: Patagonia's empathetic leadership is evident in its employee-centered policies, which include flexible work schedules, generous parental leave, and on-site childcare. The company recognizes that employees have lives outside of work and provides the flexibility and support needed to balance their personal and professional responsibilities.

Patagonia also invests heavily in employee development, offering opportunities for training, mentorship, and growth. The company's leadership encourages employees to pursue their passions and develop new skills, whether related to their current role or in preparation for future opportunities. Patagonia's empathetic approach to leadership extends to its environmental and social initiatives, which align with the values of many of its employees.

Outcome: Patagonia's empathetic leadership has led to high levels of employee engagement, loyalty, and satisfaction. The company consistently ranks as one of the best places to work, and its employees are deeply committed to its mission. Patagonia's success demonstrates that prioritizing empathy and employee well-being can lead to long-term business success, as well as positive social and environmental impact.

The case studies in this chapter illustrate the transformative power of empathetic leadership across a range of industries and contexts. From crisis management and organizational change to innovation and employee development, empathy has proven to be a key driver of success. By understanding the needs, emotions, and perspectives of their teams and stakeholders, empathetic leaders are able to create more inclusive, supportive, and effective organizations.

As these examples demonstrate, empathy is not just a soft skill but a strategic leadership tool that can lead to improved performance, innovation, and employee satisfaction.

CHAPTER EIGHT

CULTIVATING EMPATHY AS A LEADER – PRACTICAL STRATEGIES FOR DAILY LEADERSHIP

Empathy is an essential component of effective leadership, yet it is not always easy to cultivate or sustain. It requires continuous self-awareness, practice, and intentionality. Leaders who seek to lead with empathy must understand how to actively integrate it into their day-to-day interactions and decision-making processes. This chapter outlines actionable strategies for developing empathy as a core leadership skill, along with tips for maintaining empathy even in the most challenging situations.

By committing to the daily practice of empathy, leaders can foster a more inclusive and supportive environment, inspire loyalty, and drive performance in a way that aligns with the well-being of their team members. Empathy is not just a leadership trait but a transformative approach that requires a deep understanding of human dynamics.

Understanding the Challenges of Empathetic Leadership

Before diving into specific strategies, it's important to recognize the challenges that empathetic leaders may face. While empathy can lead to stronger relationships and more effective teams, it also requires emotional investment, vulnerability, and a readiness to understand the needs and emotions of others.

Some common challenges that empathetic leaders encounter include:

1. **Emotional Fatigue**: Constantly attuning to the emotions of others can lead to emotional fatigue or burnout. Leaders must find a balance between understanding others' needs and protecting their own emotional well-being.
2. **Decision-Making Dilemmas**: Empathetic leaders often face situations where they must make tough decisions that may not align with everyone's needs. Balancing empathy with the practical needs of the organization can be difficult.
3. **Misunderstanding Empathy as Weakness**: Some leaders may worry that showing empathy will make them appear weak or indecisive. However, empathy, when used appropriately, is a strength that can create respect and loyalty from the team.
4. **Empathy Versus Action**: Empathy must be combined with action. Understanding others' feelings is important, but leaders must also take steps to address those feelings and create solutions that benefit both individuals and the organization.

Daily Practices for Cultivating Empathy

Empathy is a skill that can be developed with consistent effort. Below are some practical strategies that leaders can implement daily to ensure they are leading with empathy.

1. **Active Listening**

Active listening is one of the most fundamental components of empathetic leadership. It goes beyond hearing what someone says; it involves truly understanding the emotions, concerns, and perspectives behind their words. Leaders who practice active listening are more likely to build trust, create open lines of communication, and demonstrate that they value their team members' input.

- **How to Practice Active Listening**: When engaging in conversations with team members, set aside distractions and focus entirely on the person speaking. Show that you are listening by maintaining eye contact, nodding, and asking clarifying questions to demonstrate your understanding. Avoid interrupting or jumping to conclusions.
- **Active Listening in Practice**: For example, during one-on-one meetings, allow your team members to express their thoughts fully before offering your own input. Paraphrase their key points to ensure you have understood their perspective and validate their feelings by acknowledging their challenges or concerns.

2. **Practicing Mindfulness**

Mindfulness can help leaders stay present in their interactions with others, allowing them to approach situations with clarity and compassion. By cultivating mindfulness, leaders can better manage their emotions, reduce stress, and remain attuned to the needs of their team members.

- **How to Practice Mindfulness**: Start each day with a short mindfulness exercise, such as meditation or deep breathing. This helps to center your thoughts and approach the day with greater focus and calmness. Throughout the day, take small pauses before entering meetings or making decisions to ground yourself and ensure you are responding, not reacting.
- **Mindfulness in Practice**: When a conflict arises within your team, take a moment to breathe and reflect on the emotions involved. This will help you respond with empathy rather than reacting impulsively. For instance, if a team member is frustrated, mindfulness can help you understand their frustration without becoming defensive.

3. **Regular Check-Ins**

Empathetic leaders regularly check in with their team members to gauge their well-being and understand their challenges. These check-ins can be formal, such as one-on-one meetings, or informal, like a casual conversation over coffee. The goal is to create a space where team members feel comfortable sharing their concerns and receiving support.

- **How to Implement Regular Check-Ins**: Schedule recurring one-on-one meetings with each team member to discuss their work progress, challenges, and personal well-being. Be sure to ask open-ended questions, such as "How are you

feeling about your current workload?" or "Is there anything you wish bolster with?"
- **Check-Ins in Practice**: In a fast-paced work environment, regular check-ins allow leaders to catch issues early before they become bigger problems. For example, if a team member is feeling overwhelmed, a timely check-in can help the leader adjust their workload or provide additional support.

4. **Creating Psychological Safety**

Psychological safety is the belief that one can express themselves without fear of negative consequences. In an empathetic leadership environment, team members feel safe to speak openly, share their ideas, and admit to mistakes without the fear of judgment or retribution.

- **How to Foster Psychological Safety**: Lead by example by admitting your own mistakes, showing vulnerability, and encouraging open dialogue. Be sure to provide constructive feedback in a way that fosters growth rather than instilling fear. Reward and recognize team members who take risks or offer new ideas, even if they don't always succeed.
- **Psychological Safety in Practice**: When a team member makes a mistake, instead of focusing on blame, use the opportunity to engage in a learning conversation. Ask questions like, "What did we learn from this?" and "How can we prevent this in the future?" This approach builds trust and fosters a culture of growth rather than fear.

5. Incorporating Empathy into Decision-Making

Empathy should be a guiding factor in leadership decisions, especially when those decisions impact the well-being of the team. By considering how decisions will affect others emotionally and practically, leaders can make more informed, compassionate choices.

- **How to Use Empathy in Decision-Making**: Before making a decision, put yourself in the shoes of those who will be affected. Ask yourself how the decision will impact them, both in the short term and long term. Consider holding team discussions to gather diverse perspectives before reaching a conclusion.
- **Empathy in Decision-Making Practice**: For example, when deciding whether to implement a new policy, such as flexible working hours, a leader might consult with their team to understand their personal needs. While some employees may appreciate the flexibility, others may find it difficult to manage. Empathetic leaders weigh these perspectives before making decisions.

6. Building Emotional Intelligence

Emotional intelligence (EQ) is closely tied to empathy and is critical for effective leadership. It involves recognizing and understanding your own emotions, as well as those of others, and using this awareness to manage relationships and navigate social complexities.

- **How to Build Emotional Intelligence**: Regularly reflect on your emotional reactions to

situations and consider how they may affect your interactions with others. Practice self-regulation by managing your emotions, especially in high-pressure situations. Empathize with others by identifying their emotions and responding in a way that acknowledges their feelings.
- **Emotional Intelligence in Practice**: Suppose a team member reacts negatively to constructive criticism. Rather than responding defensively, emotionally intelligent leaders would recognize that the individual may feel embarrassed or overwhelmed. They would approach the situation with compassion, offering additional support or encouragement to help the team member recover and grow.

Developing Empathy as a Long-Term Leadership Practice

Empathy is not a one-time action but a long-term leadership practice that requires continuous development. Below are some strategies that can help leaders sustain empathy over the course of their careers.

1. **Engage in Continuous Learning**

Empathetic leaders are always learning and growing, particularly in understanding the diverse perspectives of others. Continuous learning about emotional intelligence, diversity, equity, and inclusion can help leaders broaden their understanding of the experiences of those around them.

- **How to Engage in Continuous Learning**: Attend workshops, read books, or take courses that focus on emotional intelligence, leadership development, and diversity and inclusion. Engage in conversations with people from different backgrounds to expand your understanding of various perspectives.
- **Continuous Learning in Practice**: For instance, a leader may take a course on unconscious bias to better understand how biases can affect decision-making and team dynamics. This learning can help them become more empathetic and inclusive in their leadership approach.

2. **Seek Feedback**

Leaders who are committed to developing empathy should seek feedback from their teams and peers about how they are perceived. This feedback provides valuable insights into areas where the leader may need to improve and can help them identify blind spots in their empathetic practices.

- **How to Seek Feedback**: Create a culture where feedback is welcomed and regularly sought. Encourage your team to provide honest feedback, whether through formal surveys, one-on-one conversations, or anonymous channels.
- **Feedback in Practice**: After a major project, a leader might ask their team, "How did my leadership during this project impact you? Are there any areas where I can improve in supporting you?" This criticism can uncover whether the pioneer

is really practicing sympathy and where they might have to be alter.

3. **Practice Self-Care**

Empathy can be emotionally taxing, especially for leaders who are consistently managing the needs and emotions of others. Practicing self-care is essential for maintaining the emotional energy needed to lead with empathy. Leaders must prioritize their own well-being to ensure they are able to show up for their team in a supportive and empathetic way.

- **How to Practice Self-Care**: Schedule regular breaks, engage in activities that bring you joy, and establish boundaries between work and personal life. Take time to recharge by spending time with loved ones or engaging in hobbies that relax and rejuvenate you.
- **Self-Care in Practice**: For example, a leader who practices self-care might block out time on their calendar each week for physical activity, meditation, or spending time outdoors. By taking care of their own well-being, they ensure they can continue to lead with empathy and compassion.

Empathy is a critical leadership skill that requires practice, commitment, and a willingness to continually evolve. By integrating empathy into daily interactions, decision-making, and organizational practices, leaders can create a more inclusive, supportive, and successful work environment.

As this chapter has illustrated, cultivating empathy is not an overnight process but a long-term leadership journey.

It involves active listening, mindfulness, psychological safety, and emotional intelligence. Leaders who embrace these practices can build stronger relationships with their teams, foster innovation, and inspire loyalty, leading to more positive outcomes for both the organization and its employees.

CHAPTER NINE

EMBEDDING EMPATHY INTO ORGANIZATIONAL CULTURE

Empathy is not just a leadership trait; it's a value that can transform an entire organization. To truly thrive, empathy must go beyond individual leadership practices and be woven into the fabric of the organization's culture. This chapter explores the steps leaders can take to embed empathy into organizational culture and create an environment where empathy is practiced at all levels of the company. We will examine how policies, processes, and daily interactions can reflect and reinforce empathy, ultimately leading to better employee engagement, innovation, and business outcomes.

Embedding empathy into organizational culture is a long-term effort that requires commitment from leadership and buy-in from all employees. When empathy becomes a core value of the organization, it influences decision-making, communication, and the overall employee experience. This chapter will cover specific strategies to help organizations foster a culture of empathy and measure its impact.

The Importance of Organizational Culture in Shaping Behavior

Organizational culture is the set of shared values, beliefs, and practices that influence how employees interact with each other, approach their work, and engage with customers. A positive culture can foster collaboration, innovation, and trust, while a toxic culture can lead to disengagement, high turnover, and poor performance.

Empathy plays a critical role in shaping a healthy organizational culture. When empathy is prioritized, employees feel valued and understood, which leads to stronger relationships, higher levels of trust, and a more supportive work environment. A culture rooted in empathy encourages open communication, reduces conflicts, and enables teams to work more effectively together.

The Business Case for an Empathetic Culture

Before diving into the strategies for embedding empathy, it's important to understand why fostering an empathetic culture is good for business. Organizations that cultivate empathy tend to see improvements in several key areas:

1. **Employee Engagement and Retention**: Employees who feel understood and supported are more likely to be engaged in their work and remain loyal to the company. Empathy helps create a positive work environment, where employees are motivated to contribute their best efforts.
2. **Productivity and Innovation**: A culture of empathy encourages open communication and psychological safety, which are essential for creativity and innovation. Employees who feel safe expressing their ideas are more likely to propose new solutions, experiment, and take risks, leading to higher levels of innovation.
3. **Customer Satisfaction**: Empathy within the organization extends to customer interactions.

Companies that practice empathy internally are more likely to deliver empathetic customer service, leading to higher levels of customer satisfaction and loyalty.
4. **Attraction of Top Talent**: Organizations known for their empathetic culture attract top talent who value an inclusive and supportive work environment. As the workforce becomes increasingly diverse and values-driven, empathy becomes a key differentiator in attracting and retaining high-performing employees.
5. **Financial Performance**: Companies with empathetic cultures often outperform their peers financially. Research shows that organizations with engaged, satisfied employees tend to have higher profitability, as their teams are more productive and motivated to achieve company goals.

Key Strategies for Embedding Empathy into Organizational Culture

1. **Leadership Commitment and Role Modeling**

The first step in embedding empathy into organizational culture is ensuring that leaders at all levels are committed to practicing and promoting empathy. Leadership sets the tone for the entire organization, and employees look to their leaders for cues on how to behave. When leaders consistently demonstrate empathy in their interactions, decision-making, and communication, it sends a clear message that empathy is a valued trait within the organization.

- **How to Implement**: Leaders should model empathy through active listening, open communication, and understanding others' perspectives. They should also take responsibility for fostering a culture where empathy is encouraged. This includes providing mentorship and coaching to other leaders and managers on how to practice empathy.
- **Example**: Consider a leader who, during a company-wide meeting, takes time to acknowledge the emotional challenges employees may be facing during a difficult period, such as an organizational restructuring or external crisis. By acknowledging these emotions and offering support, the leader sets an empathetic tone for the organization.

2. **Hiring for Empathy**

To build a culture of empathy, it's important to hire individuals who possess strong empathetic skills and who align with the organization's values. This doesn't mean that empathy should be the only criterion for hiring, but it should be considered alongside other important qualities, such as technical skills and experience.

- **How to Implement**: During the recruitment process, integrate empathy into job descriptions and interviews. Ask candidates questions that reveal their ability to understand others' perspectives, communicate effectively, and navigate complex emotional dynamics. Additionally, emphasize the importance of empathy in your company's culture and values during the interview process.

- **Example**: A company might ask candidates to describe a time when they had to navigate a difficult conversation with a colleague or resolve a conflict. The goal is to assess how they approached the situation and whether they used empathy to understand the other person's perspective and find a solution.

3. **Training and Development Programs**

Sympathy, like every expertise, can be created with hone.. Providing ongoing training and development opportunities focused on empathy and emotional intelligence helps employees at all levels build the skills they need to create an empathetic work environment.

- **How to Implement**: Offer workshops, seminars, and online courses that focus on empathy, active listening, emotional intelligence, and conflict resolution. Make these programs available to all employees, from entry-level workers to senior leaders. In addition to formal training, consider incorporating empathy exercises into team meetings or leadership development programs.
- **Example**: A company could organize a training session that teaches employees how to actively listen to their colleagues and respond empathetically to difficult situations. During the session, employees could participate in role-playing exercises that allow them to practice empathetic responses in real-world scenarios.

4. **Recognizing and Rewarding Empathy**

To reinforce empathy as a core organizational value, it's important to recognize and reward employees who demonstrate empathetic behaviors. This not only encourages others to follow suit but also signals that empathy is a valued trait within the organization.

- **How to Implement**: Create a recognition program that highlights empathetic behaviors and contributions. This could take the form of peer-to-peer recognition, where employees nominate each other for demonstrating empathy, or leadership recognition, where managers acknowledge and celebrate empathetic actions.
- **Example**: An organization might implement a "Compassionate Colleague" award, where employees can nominate their peers who have gone above and beyond to support others. The award could be given quarterly, with winners recognized in company-wide meetings or newsletters.

5. **Empathetic Policies and Procedures**

Company policies and procedures should reflect the organization's commitment to empathy. This includes policies around work-life balance, diversity and inclusion, employee support, and conflict resolution. Empathetic policies signal to employees that their well-being is a priority and that the company is committed to understanding and addressing their needs.

- **How to Implement**: Review existing policies and identify areas where empathy can be better integrated. For example, ensure that your company's parental leave policy is supportive of new parents, or that your conflict resolution process allows for employees to voice their concerns in a safe and supportive environment. Additionally, consider creating policies that encourage flexible work arrangements or mental health support.
- **Example**: A company might introduce a "wellness day" policy, allowing employees to take a day off for mental health or personal reasons without the need to provide a detailed explanation. This policy demonstrates empathy by recognizing that employees may need time to recharge and take care of their well-being.

6. **Creating Inclusive Spaces for Open Dialogue**

A culture of empathy thrives when employees feel safe to express their thoughts, emotions, and concerns without fear of judgment or retaliation. Creating inclusive spaces for open dialogue helps foster psychological safety, allowing employees to communicate openly and honestly with their colleagues and leaders.

- **How to Implement**: Encourage regular check-ins, one-on-one meetings, and team discussions where employees can share their thoughts and feelings in a supportive environment. Consider implementing anonymous feedback mechanisms, such as suggestion boxes or employee surveys, to

give employees additional ways to voice their concerns.
- **Example**: An organization might host regular "listening sessions," where employees are invited to share their perspectives on workplace issues, challenges, or successes. These sessions are facilitated by a neutral party and designed to create a space where employees feel comfortable expressing their emotions and opinions.

7. **Encouraging Cross-Departmental Collaboration**

Empathy is strengthened when employees have the opportunity to collaborate with colleagues from different departments and backgrounds. Cross-departmental collaboration encourages employees to step outside their own perspective and understand the experiences and challenges of others in the organization.

- **How to Implement**: Create opportunities for employees from different departments to work together on projects, participate in task forces, or engage in team-building activities. Ensure that these collaborations are designed to foster understanding and mutual respect between team members.
- **Example**: A company might establish a cross-departmental innovation team tasked with developing new product ideas. The team could include members from marketing, sales, research and development, and customer service. Through collaboration, team members gain a deeper

understanding of each other's roles and how they contribute to the organization's success.

8. **Empathy in Customer Interactions**

Embedding empathy into organizational culture also means extending it to customer interactions. When employees treat customers with empathy, it not only enhances customer satisfaction but also reinforces empathy as a core value within the organization.

- **How to Implement**: Train employees, particularly those in customer-facing roles, to approach customer interactions with empathy. This includes listening to customers' needs, understanding their pain points, and responding in a compassionate and solution-oriented manner. Empower employees to take action when they encounter a customer in need, even if it requires going beyond standard procedures.
- **Example**: Consider a customer service representative who goes out of their way to help a frustrated customer resolve an issue, taking extra time to listen to their concerns and offering a personalized solution. This empathetic approach not only improves the customer experience but also reinforces the organization's commitment to empathy.

Measuring the Impact of an Empathetic Culture

To ensure that empathy is truly embedded into the culture, organizations should regularly assess the impact of their efforts. This may be done through a combination of subjective and quantitative measures.

- **Employee Engagement Surveys**: Regularly survey employees to gauge their perceptions of the organization's culture, leadership, and levels of empathy. Use these surveys to identify areas for improvement and track progress over time.
- **Turnover and Retention Rates**: Monitor employee turnover and retention rates to assess whether a culture of empathy is contributing to higher employee satisfaction and lower attrition.
- **Customer Feedback**: Collect customer feedback to determine whether employees' empathetic behaviors are leading to higher levels of customer satisfaction and loyalty.
- **Peer and Manager Feedback**: Encourage peer-to-peer and manager feedback to assess how well employees are practicing empathy in their daily interactions.

Embedding empathy into organizational culture requires a thoughtful, consistent approach. It starts with leadership but must extend to every aspect of the organization, from hiring and training to policies, communication, and customer interactions. By making empathy a core value, organizations can create a more inclusive, supportive, and high-performing environment that benefits employees, customers, and the business as a whole.

CHAPTER TEN

SUSTAINING EMPATHY IN LEADERSHIP AND ORGANIZATIONAL GROWTH

As we've explored in previous chapters, embedding empathy into leadership and organizational culture is crucial for fostering a thriving work environment. But beyond the initial steps of cultivating and integrating empathy, one of the greatest challenges lies in sustaining it over time—particularly as organizations grow, face new challenges, or adapt to changing market conditions. How can leaders ensure that empathy continues to be a foundational value, and that it remains integrated into decision-making processes, daily interactions, and company policies?

This chapter will delve into the strategies that leaders can employ to maintain empathy as a guiding principle in leadership, regardless of the company's size or the challenges it faces. We'll also look at real-world examples of organizations that have successfully sustained empathy and explore the ways that empathy can help drive long-term success in areas such as innovation, employee satisfaction, and financial performance.

The Challenges of Sustaining Empathy in Growth and Change

Growth and change are inevitable for any organization that seeks to remain competitive and relevant. Whether it's expanding into new markets, scaling operations, or responding to technological advancements, companies are constantly evolving. However, these periods of growth and change can sometimes challenge the foundational values that were put in place during the company's early stages. As teams grow and structures become more complex, maintaining a focus on empathy requires conscious effort and strategic action.

Here are some common challenges organizations face when trying to sustain empathy during growth:

1. **Increased Complexity**: As organizations grow, they become more complex, with additional layers of hierarchy, increased specialization, and more geographically dispersed teams. This complexity can make it difficult for leaders to maintain close, empathetic relationships with all employees.
2. **Pressure to Scale Quickly**: Rapid growth can place significant pressure on leaders to prioritize efficiency and speed over interpersonal connection. While scaling a business often requires process optimization and a focus on key performance indicators (KPIs), it's important not to lose sight of the human element.
3. **Cultural Drift**: As new employees join the organization, the original culture may begin to shift. Without deliberate action to maintain empathy as a core value, cultural drift can occur, where the organization's initial commitment to empathy is diluted over time.
4. **Focus on Profitability**: Financial pressures can sometimes lead to tough decisions, including cost-cutting measures, workforce reductions, or restructuring. In these situations, leaders may feel torn between maintaining empathetic leadership

and making decisions that are necessary for the financial health of the company.
5. **Leadership Turnover**: Leadership transitions can also pose a challenge to sustaining empathy. When new leaders come into the organization, they may bring different values and priorities, potentially disrupting the culture of empathy that has been established.

Despite these challenges, sustaining empathy is not only possible but essential for long-term success. The key is for leaders to be intentional about integrating empathy into every aspect of the organization, from strategic decision-making to everyday interactions. Let's explore some strategies that can help leaders sustain empathy in the face of growth and change.

Strategies for Sustaining Empathy in Leadership

1. **Institutionalize Empathy Through Policies and Practices**

One of the most effective ways to sustain empathy in leadership is by institutionalizing it through formal policies and practices. When empathy is embedded in the organization's policies, it becomes a standard operating procedure rather than an optional behavior. This ensures that empathy is consistently practiced across the organization, even as it grows and evolves.

- **How to Implement**: Leaders should work with HR and other departments to develop policies that reflect the organization's commitment to empathy. This could include policies around diversity and

inclusion, flexible work arrangements, mental health support, and conflict resolution. Additionally, empathy should be incorporated into performance reviews, leadership development programs, and employee feedback processes.
- **Example**: A tech company may implement a policy that encourages flexible work hours to accommodate employees with caregiving responsibilities. By institutionalizing flexibility, the company demonstrates its commitment to understanding and supporting the personal needs of its employees.

2. **Empathy as a Core Leadership Competency**

Empathy should not be viewed as a "nice-to-have" quality but as a core leadership competency. Leaders who prioritize empathy are better equipped to build trust, foster collaboration, and navigate complex interpersonal dynamics. By integrating empathy into leadership development programs, organizations can ensure that their leaders have the skills and mindset needed to lead with compassion and understanding.

- **How to Implement**: Develop training programs that focus on empathy, emotional intelligence, and active listening for leaders at all levels. Make empathy a key criterion in leadership assessments, promotions, and hiring decisions. Additionally, provide leaders with tools and resources to practice empathy in their daily interactions with employees, customers, and stakeholders.
- **Example**: A global consulting firm might offer leadership training that includes workshops on

empathetic communication, conflict resolution, and understanding different cultural perspectives. Leaders who complete this training are better equipped to lead diverse teams with empathy and respect.

3. **Build Empathy into Decision-Making Processes**

In fast-paced, high-stakes environments, leaders often have to make difficult decisions under pressure. While it's tempting to focus solely on data, numbers, and KPIs, it's important for leaders to incorporate empathy into the decision-making process. By considering the impact of decisions on employees, customers, and other stakeholders, leaders can make more informed and compassionate choices.

- **How to Implement**: When making decisions, leaders should take time to gather input from those who will be affected by the outcome. This could involve conducting employee surveys, holding town hall meetings, or consulting with team leaders. Additionally, leaders should practice empathy by considering how their decisions will affect the well-being, morale, and productivity of their teams.
- **Example**: When considering a major restructuring, a company might hold a series of listening sessions with employees to gather feedback on how the changes will impact their work and personal lives. By incorporating this feedback into the final decision, the company demonstrates empathy and ensures that employees feel heard and valued.

4. **Empathy in Performance Metrics**

To sustain empathy over the long term, it's important to measure and reward it as part of the organization's performance metrics. This reinforces the message that empathy is a key driver of success and encourages leaders and employees alike to prioritize empathetic behaviors.

- **How to Implement**: Incorporate empathy into performance reviews, employee recognition programs, and leadership assessments. For example, leaders could be evaluated not only on their ability to meet financial targets but also on their ability to foster a positive work environment, build strong relationships, and support the well-being of their teams.
- **Example**: An organization might introduce a 360-degree feedback system where employees provide input on their managers' empathy and emotional intelligence. This feedback is then incorporated into the manager's overall performance evaluation.

5. **Fostering a Culture of Psychological Safety**

Psychological safety is the belief that one can express ideas, ask questions, and take risks without fear of punishment or judgment. It's a critical component of sustaining empathy in leadership because it encourages open communication, vulnerability, and trust. When employees feel psychologically safe, they are more likely to share their concerns, provide honest feedback, and collaborate effectively.

- **How to Implement**: Leaders should actively work to create a culture of psychological safety by encouraging open dialogue, listening without judgment, and responding to feedback with empathy. This can be achieved through regular one-on-one meetings, team check-ins, and creating spaces where employees feel comfortable discussing their challenges and emotions.
- **Example**: A manager who leads with empathy might start each team meeting with an open check-in, where employees are invited to share how they are feeling, both personally and professionally. By creating a safe space for these conversations, the manager fosters trust and empathy within the team.

6. **Leverage Technology to Sustain Empathy**

In today's digital age, technology can play a powerful role in helping organizations sustain empathy, especially in remote or hybrid work environments. Tools such as employee engagement platforms, virtual meeting software, and anonymous feedback systems can help leaders stay connected with their teams and monitor their well-being.

- **How to Implement**: Use technology to facilitate regular check-ins, gather employee feedback, and provide virtual support. Additionally, leaders should be mindful of how they use technology to communicate. While digital communication tools are efficient, they should not replace meaningful, empathetic interactions. Leaders should strive to

balance the convenience of technology with the need for human connection.
- **Example**: A company with a remote workforce might use an employee engagement platform to send out regular pulse surveys that check in on employees' mental health, job satisfaction, and overall well-being. The results of these surveys are then used to inform leadership decisions and ensure that employees are receiving the support they need.

Real-World Examples of Sustaining Empathy in Leadership

1. **Patagonia: Leading with Empathy and Environmental Responsibility**

Patagonia, the outdoor clothing company, is often cited as a leader in corporate empathy, not only for its treatment of employees but also for its commitment to environmental sustainability. Patagonia's leadership has sustained empathy by embedding it into the company's mission and business practices. Employees are encouraged to take time off to participate in environmental activism, and the company has created flexible work policies to support work-life balance. By aligning its values with empathy, Patagonia has built a loyal employee base and a strong brand reputation.

2. **Microsoft: Empathy in Action Under Satya Nadella's Leadership**

When Satya Nadella became CEO of Microsoft in 2014, he made empathy a cornerstone of his leadership approach.

Nadella's commitment to empathy has been credited with transforming Microsoft's culture, fostering greater collaboration, innovation, and employee engagement. One of the ways Nadella sustained empathy in leadership was by encouraging a "growth mindset" within the company—a belief that individuals can grow and develop through effort and learning. By focusing on empathy and learning, Nadella helped Microsoft regain its competitive edge while maintaining a positive, supportive work environment.

3. **Airbnb: Empathy in a Crisis**

In 2020, as the COVID-19 pandemic led to a sharp decline in travel, Airbnb faced significant financial challenges. The company had to create the troublesome choice to lay off a parcel of its workforce. However, CEO Brian Chesky handled the situation with empathy, providing generous severance packages, extended healthcare benefits, and job placement assistance to those affected. Chesky also communicated transparently with employees throughout the process, acknowledging the emotional toll of the layoffs and expressing gratitude for their contributions. By leading with empathy during a crisis, Chesky helped preserve Airbnb's culture and employee trust.

Empathy as a Driver of Long-Term Success

Empathy is not only a leadership skill; it's a strategic advantage. Organizations that prioritize empathy tend to outperform their competitors in several key areas, including innovation, employee engagement, and customer satisfaction. Over the long term, empathy helps organizations build stronger, more resilient teams that can navigate challenges with agility and compassion.

Here are some ways empathy drives long-term success:

1. **Fostering Innovation**: Empathy encourages creativity by creating an environment where employees feel safe to share new ideas and take risks. By understanding the needs and challenges of customers and employees, leaders can identify new opportunities for innovation and growth.
2. **Building Employee Loyalty**: Empathetic leadership leads to higher levels of employee satisfaction and retention. Workers who feel esteemed and caught on are more likely to remain with the company, decreasing turnover and related costs.
3. **Enhancing Customer Loyalty**: Companies that lead with empathy tend to have stronger relationships with their customers. When employees treat customers with compassion and understanding, it leads to higher levels of customer satisfaction, loyalty, and repeat business.
4. **Strengthening Organizational Resilience**: In times of crisis, empathy helps organizations maintain trust, transparency, and morale. Leaders who communicate with empathy during difficult times can keep teams motivated and focused, even when facing uncertainty.

Sustaining empathy in leadership is an ongoing process that requires commitment, intention, and action. By embedding empathy into organizational policies, decision-making processes, and leadership development programs, companies can ensure that empathy remains a core value, even as they grow and evolve. The benefits of sustained empathy are clear: higher employee engagement, stronger customer relationships, and long-term business success.

CHAPTER ELEVEN

CREATING A LEGACY OF EMPATHY IN LEADERSHIP

As organizations evolve and new generations of leaders emerge, the values and practices that have been established need to be passed on to ensure continuity and growth. Empathy, as a cornerstone of effective leadership, must be nurtured and sustained to create a lasting impact on organizational culture and success. This chapter delves into how leaders can create a legacy of empathy, focusing on mentorship, succession planning, leadership development, and the role of organizational values in shaping future leaders.

The Importance of a Leadership Legacy

A leadership legacy encompasses the values, practices, and principles that leaders pass down to future generations. It shapes the organization's culture, influences employee behavior, and impacts the long-term success of the business. Creating a legacy of empathy is crucial because it ensures that future leaders continue to prioritize compassion, understanding, and connection in their roles. An empathetic legacy not only fosters a supportive work environment but also drives sustainable business outcomes by enhancing employee engagement, customer satisfaction, and organizational resilience.

Key Components of a Leadership Legacy:

1. **Values and Principles**: Core beliefs and ethical standards that guide decision-making and behavior.

2. **Culture and Practices**: Organizational norms and practices that reflect and reinforce the values.
3. **Talent Development**: The investment in mentoring and developing future leaders to continue the legacy.
4. **Impact and Influence**: The effect of the leadership style on organizational performance and employee well-being.

Mentorship: Passing on the Empathy Skillset

Mentorship is a critical component of creating a legacy of empathy. Effective mentors not only provide guidance and support but also model empathetic behavior, helping mentees develop their own empathetic skills. By investing time and effort into mentoring, experienced leaders can instill a culture of empathy in the next generation of leaders.

Strategies for Effective Mentorship:

1. **Model Empathetic Behavior**: Mentors should demonstrate empathy through their actions and interactions. This includes active listening, providing constructive feedback, and showing understanding in challenging situations. By modeling these behaviors, mentors set an example for mentees to follow.
2. **Provide Constructive Feedback**: Feedback is an essential part of mentorship. It should be delivered with empathy, focusing on growth and development rather than criticism. Constructive feedback helps mentees understand their strengths

and areas for improvement while feeling valued and supported.
3. **Encourage Reflection**: Mentors should encourage mentees to reflect on their experiences and interactions. Reflection helps mentees develop self-awareness and a deeper understanding of how empathy can be applied in different contexts.
4. **Support Personal and Professional Growth**: Mentors should support their mentees' personal and professional development by offering guidance, resources, and opportunities for learning. This includes helping mentees set goals, navigate challenges, and build skills necessary for empathetic leadership.

Example of Mentorship in Action: A senior leader at a technology company might mentor a young manager by providing regular one-on-one meetings where they discuss leadership challenges and opportunities. The mentor shares personal experiences, offers guidance on handling difficult situations with empathy, and provides feedback on the manager's approach to team interactions. The mentor also encourages the manager to seek feedback from their team and reflect on their leadership style.

Succession Planning: Ensuring Continuity of Empathy

Succession planning is the process of identifying and developing internal talent to fill key leadership roles in the future. Effective succession planning ensures that the values and practices of current leaders, including empathy, are carried forward. By preparing future leaders to take on critical roles, organizations can maintain continuity in their leadership style and culture.

Key Aspects of Succession Planning for Empathy:

1. **Identify Potential Leaders**: Organizations should identify individuals who demonstrate the potential to lead with empathy. This includes assessing their interpersonal skills, emotional intelligence, and ability to build relationships.
2. **Develop Empathetic Skills**: Provide development opportunities focused on empathy and emotional intelligence. This includes training programs, workshops, and coaching that help potential leaders build the skills necessary for empathetic leadership.
3. **Create Development Plans**: Develop individualized plans for potential leaders that outline the skills and experiences they need to gain. These plans should include opportunities for mentorship, cross-functional projects, and leadership roles.
4. **Evaluate and Adjust**: Regularly evaluate the progress of potential leaders and adjust development plans as needed. This ensures that individuals are on track to assume leadership roles and continue the legacy of empathy.

Example of Succession Planning in Action: A multinational corporation may implement a formal succession planning program that identifies high-potential employees for leadership roles. These individuals receive targeted training on empathetic leadership, participate in mentoring programs, and are given opportunities to lead cross-functional teams. Regular evaluations ensure that these employees are developing the skills needed to lead with empathy and align with the company's values.

Leadership Development: Cultivating Future Empathetic Leaders

Leadership development programs play a crucial role in cultivating future leaders who are capable of sustaining a culture of empathy. These programs should be designed to build both the technical and interpersonal skills required for effective leadership.

Components of Leadership Development for Empathy:

1. **Training on Emotional Intelligence**: Incorporate training programs that focus on developing emotional intelligence, including self-awareness, self-regulation, empathy, and social skills. This training helps leaders understand their own emotions and the emotions of others.
2. **Experiential Learning**: Use experiential learning techniques, such as role-playing, simulations, and real-world projects, to help leaders practice empathetic behaviors in a controlled environment. This hands-on approach allows leaders to apply their skills and receive feedback.
3. **Feedback and Reflection**: Provide regular feedback and opportunities for reflection to help leaders assess their empathetic skills and identify areas for improvement. This feedback can come from mentors, peers, or direct reports.

4. **Peer Learning and Collaboration**: Encourage peer learning and collaboration by creating opportunities for leaders to share experiences, discuss challenges, and learn from each other. This collaborative approach fosters a culture of mutual support and empathy.

Example of Leadership Development in Action: An organization might implement a leadership development program that includes workshops on emotional intelligence, experiential learning modules, and regular feedback sessions. Leaders participate in group discussions where they share their experiences and learn from their peers. They also receive coaching and mentoring to help them apply empathetic leadership principles in their roles.

Embedding Empathy into Organizational Values

Organizational values are the guiding principles that shape the company's culture and behavior. To create a lasting legacy of empathy, organizations must ensure that empathy is embedded into their core values and reflected in their everyday practices.

Steps to Embed Empathy into Organizational Values:

1. **Define Core Values**: Clearly define empathy as a core value within the organization's mission and vision statements. Ensure that these values are communicated effectively to all employees and stakeholders.

2. **Integrate Values into Policies and Procedures**: Align organizational policies and procedures with the core values of empathy. This includes hiring practices, performance evaluations, and employee support programs.
3. **Promote Values Through Communication**: Regularly communicate the importance of empathy and the organization's commitment to it. Use internal communications, such as newsletters, town hall meetings, and leadership messages, to reinforce the values.
4. **Celebrate and Reward Empathy**: Recognize and reward employees who exemplify empathetic behavior. This can be done through formal recognition programs, awards, and public acknowledgment.

Example of Embedding Empathy into Organizational Values: A nonprofit organization might include empathy as a core value in its mission statement and ensure that it is reflected in all aspects of the organization's operations. The organization might implement policies that support work-life balance, provide training on empathetic communication, and recognize employees who go above and beyond to support their colleagues and communities.

Measuring the Impact of Empathy

To ensure that empathy remains a lasting legacy, organizations must measure its impact on various aspects of the business. This involves assessing how empathy influences employee engagement, customer satisfaction, and overall organizational performance.

Methods for Measuring the Impact of Empathy:

1. **Employee Surveys and Feedback**: Use employee surveys and feedback mechanisms to assess perceptions of empathy within the organization. Measure factors such as job satisfaction, morale, and the effectiveness of leadership.
2. **Customer Satisfaction Metrics**: Evaluate customer satisfaction and loyalty to determine how empathetic interactions impact customer experiences. Use metrics such as Net Promoter Scores (NPS) and customer feedback surveys.
3. **Performance and Productivity Data**: Analyze performance and productivity data to assess the impact of empathetic leadership on organizational outcomes. Look for correlations between empathetic behaviors and key performance indicators.
4. **Retention and Turnover Rates**: Monitor employee retention and turnover rates to assess whether a culture of empathy contributes to higher employee loyalty and lower attrition.

Example of Measuring Impact: A company might conduct regular employee engagement surveys to gauge how well employees feel supported and valued. They might also track customer satisfaction scores to understand the impact of empathetic customer service on loyalty. By analyzing these metrics, the company can determine whether their efforts to sustain empathy are achieving the desired outcomes.

Challenges and Solutions in Creating a Legacy of Empathy

While creating a legacy of empathy is essential, it comes with its own set of challenges. Organizations must be prepared to address these challenges and find solutions to ensure that empathy remains a core value.

Common Challenges:

1. **Resistance to Change**: Employees or leaders may resist changes to the organizational culture, especially if they are accustomed to different leadership styles or practices.
2. **Inconsistency in Practice**: Ensuring that empathy is consistently practiced across all levels of the organization can be challenging, particularly in large or diverse organizations.
3. **Balancing Empathy with Business Goals**: Leaders may struggle to balance empathetic practices with the need to achieve business goals and drive performance.
4. **Maintaining Empathy During Crisis**: Sustaining empathy during times of crisis or high stress can be difficult, as leaders may face competing demands and pressures.

Solutions:

1. **Communicate Clearly**: Clearly communicate the importance of empathy and the benefits it brings to the organization. Address any resistance by providing education and demonstrating the positive impact of empathetic leadership.

2. **Lead by Example**: Leaders should model empathetic behavior and hold themselves accountable for practicing empathy consistently. This sets a standard for others to take after.
3. **Align Goals and Values**: Ensure that business goals and empathetic practices are aligned by integrating empathy into strategic planning and decision-making processes.
4. **Provide Support**: Offer support and resources to help leaders and employees navigate challenges while maintaining empathy. This includes training, coaching, and access to mental health resources.

Example of Addressing Challenges: A company facing resistance to cultural changes might hold workshops and training sessions to educate employees about the benefits of empathy and provide practical strategies for integrating it into their daily work. Leaders can also share success stories and demonstrate how empathy has positively impacted the organization.

Creating a legacy of empathy in leadership is a powerful way to ensure that compassionate, understanding, and supportive practices continue to shape the organization's culture and success. By focusing on mentorship, succession planning, leadership development, and embedding empathy into organizational values, leaders can pass on a rich legacy of empathetic leadership to future generations.

CHAPTER TWELVE

THE FUTURE OF EMPATHETIC LEADERSHIP: GLOBAL PERSPECTIVES AND EMERGING TRENDS

As we look to the future, the role of empathetic leadership will continue to evolve in response to global trends, technological advancements, and changing societal expectations. This chapter explores how empathetic leadership will shape the future of work, including its impact on global perspectives, diverse communities, and the integration of new technologies. We will also examine emerging trends in leadership and how organizations can adapt to these changes while maintaining a commitment to empathy.

The Evolving Role of Empathetic Leadership

Empathetic leadership is no longer a mere option but a strategic necessity for organizations aiming to thrive in a rapidly changing world. As globalization, technological innovation, and shifting societal norms redefine the business landscape, leaders must adapt their approach to meet new challenges and opportunities. The future of empathetic leadership will be shaped by several key factors:

1. **Globalization and Cultural Diversity**

Globalization has expanded the reach of businesses, bringing together people from diverse cultural backgrounds. As organizations operate in multiple regions and interact with international stakeholders, leaders must be adept at navigating cultural differences and fostering an inclusive environment.

- **Understanding Cultural Differences**: Empathetic leaders will need to understand and respect cultural differences to build effective relationships and collaborate across borders. This includes being aware of different communication styles, customs, and expectations.
- **Promoting Inclusivity**: Leaders must actively promote inclusivity by creating a culture where diverse perspectives are valued and integrated into decision-making processes. This involves addressing biases, providing equal opportunities, and ensuring that all voices are heard.
- **Leveraging Diversity for Innovation**: Diverse teams bring varied viewpoints and experiences, which can drive innovation and creativity. Empathetic leaders should harness the power of diversity to foster a culture of collaboration and continuous improvement.

Example: A multinational company might implement cross-cultural training programs for its leaders to help them navigate cultural nuances and build relationships with international teams. Additionally, the company could establish employee resource groups to support diverse employees and promote inclusivity.

2. **Technological Advancements**

Technological advancements, including artificial intelligence (AI), automation, and digital communication tools, are transforming the way we work and interact.

Empathetic leaders will need to adapt to these changes while maintaining a human touch in their leadership approach.

- **Balancing Technology and Human Interaction**: While technology can enhance efficiency and connectivity, it's important for leaders to balance digital interactions with face-to-face communication. Empathetic leaders should use technology to support, not replace, personal connections.
- **Managing Remote and Hybrid Work**: The rise of remote and hybrid work arrangements presents new challenges for maintaining team cohesion and engagement. Empathetic leaders must find ways to support remote employees, foster collaboration, and address feelings of isolation.
- **Ethical Considerations**: As technology plays a larger role in decision-making, leaders must consider the ethical implications of their technological choices. This includes ensuring that AI and automation are used responsibly and that employees are treated fairly.

Example: A tech company might use AI-driven tools to streamline administrative tasks but also prioritize regular virtual team meetings and one-on-one check-ins to maintain personal connections with remote employees.

3. **Shifting Societal Expectations**

Societal expectations around corporate responsibility, sustainability, and social justice are evolving. Organizations are progressively held responsible for their affect on society and the environment. Empathetic leaders will need to address these expectations and lead with purpose.

- **Corporate Social Responsibility (CSR)**: Leaders should integrate CSR into the organization's core values and strategies. This includes supporting community initiatives, promoting environmental sustainability, and addressing social issues.
- **Transparency and Accountability**: Empathetic leaders must be transparent about their organization's practices and be accountable for their actions. This involves openly communicating with stakeholders and addressing concerns with honesty and integrity.
- **Supporting Employee Well-being**: As societal awareness of mental health and well-being grows, leaders must prioritize the well-being of their employees. This includes providing mental health support, work-life balance initiatives, and a supportive work environment.

Example: A retail company might launch a sustainability initiative to reduce its environmental footprint and support fair labor practices. The company could also implement programs to support employee mental health and create a positive impact in the communities it serves.

Emerging Trends in Empathetic Leadership

As the future of work continues to evolve, several emerging trends are shaping the role of empathetic leadership. Leaders who stay ahead of these trends will be better positioned to foster a positive work environment and drive organizational success.

1. **The Rise of Purpose-Driven Leadership**

Purpose-driven leadership focuses on aligning organizational goals with a broader sense of purpose beyond profit. Empathetic leaders who embrace this trend will be better equipped to inspire and engage their teams by connecting their work to a greater mission.

- **Defining Purpose**: Leaders should clearly articulate the organization's purpose and how it relates to employees' roles and contributions. This helps employees feel a sense of meaning and motivation in their work.
- **Aligning Actions with Purpose**: Empathetic leaders must ensure that the organization's actions and decisions align with its stated purpose. This includes making choices that reflect the organization's values and commitment to social responsibility.
- **Engaging Stakeholders**: Purpose-driven leaders should actively engage with stakeholders, including employees, customers, and communities, to understand their needs and expectations. This makes a difference construct believe and fortify connections.

Example: A nonprofit organization might focus on providing education and resources to underserved communities. Leaders would communicate the organization's mission clearly, align their actions with this mission, and engage with stakeholders to ensure their needs are met.

2. **The Growing Importance of Emotional Intelligence**

Emotional intelligence (EI) is becoming increasingly important in leadership as it helps leaders navigate complex interpersonal dynamics and foster positive relationships. Future leaders will need to enhance their EI to effectively manage teams and drive organizational success.

- **Developing Self-Awareness**: Leaders should work on developing self-awareness by understanding their own emotions, strengths, and weaknesses. This self-awareness helps leaders manage their reactions and build better relationships with others.
- **Building Empathy**: Empathy is a key component of EI and involves understanding and responding to others' emotions. Leaders should practice active listening, show compassion, and validate employees' feelings.
- **Managing Relationships**: Effective leaders need to manage relationships by resolving conflicts, providing support, and fostering a positive work environment. This includes addressing issues with empathy and finding solutions that benefit all parties involved.

Example: A leader in a healthcare organization might receive training on emotional intelligence to improve their ability to connect with patients and staff. This training helps the leader better understand and respond to the needs and emotions of those they serve.

3. **Focus on Employee Experience and Engagement**

The employee experience encompasses all aspects of an employee's journey within an organization, from recruitment to exit. Empathetic leaders who prioritize employee experience and engagement will create a more positive and productive work environment.

- **Enhancing the Onboarding Process**: Leaders should ensure that the onboarding process is welcoming and supportive. This includes providing clear information, offering training and resources, and making new employees feel valued.
- **Fostering a Positive Work Environment**: Empathetic leaders should create a work environment that supports employee well-being, encourages collaboration, and recognizes achievements. This includes implementing programs that enhance work-life balance and provide opportunities for growth.
- **Regular Feedback and Recognition**: Providing regular feedback and recognition helps employees feel valued and engaged. Leaders should offer constructive feedback, celebrate successes, and acknowledge employees' contributions.

Example: A software company might implement a comprehensive onboarding program that includes mentorship, training, and regular check-ins. The company could also create a recognition program that celebrates employees' achievements and contributions to the team.

4. **Embracing Diversity, Equity, and Inclusion (DEI)**

Diversity, equity, and inclusion (DEI) are becoming central to organizational culture and success. Empathetic leaders who prioritize DEI will create a more inclusive and supportive work environment that values and respects all employees.

- **Promoting Diversity**: Leaders should actively promote diversity by recruiting from a broad talent pool and ensuring that diverse perspectives are represented at all levels of the organization.
- **Ensuring Equity**: Equity involves providing equal opportunities and addressing systemic barriers that may affect certain groups. Leaders should assess and address disparities in pay, promotions, and career development.
- **Fostering Inclusion**: Inclusion means creating a culture where all employees feel welcome and valued. Leaders should implement practices that support inclusivity, such as providing training on unconscious bias and creating affinity groups.

Example: An educational institution might launch a DEI initiative that includes recruiting diverse faculty, addressing pay equity, and creating inclusive policies and practices. The institution could also provide training on unconscious bias and establish support networks for underrepresented groups.

5. **Leveraging Data and Analytics for Empathetic Leadership**

Data and analytics are increasingly used to drive decision-making and measure performance. Empathetic leaders can leverage data to gain insights into employee needs, track engagement, and assess the effectiveness of their leadership practices.

- **Collecting Employee Feedback**: Use surveys, focus groups, and other feedback mechanisms to gather information on employee satisfaction, engagement, and well-being. Analyze this information to recognize patterns and regions for enhancement.
- **Measuring Leadership Effectiveness**: Track metrics related to leadership effectiveness, such as employee turnover, productivity, and performance. Use this data to assess how well empathetic leadership practices are being implemented and their impact on the organization.
- **Driving Continuous Improvement**: Use data-driven insights to continuously improve leadership practices and create a more supportive work environment. This includes identifying best practices, addressing challenges, and making informed decisions.

Example: A financial services firm might use employee engagement surveys to gather feedback on leadership practices and analyze the data to identify areas for improvement. The firm could then implement changes based on the insights to enhance employee satisfaction and performance.

Planning for long-term: Methodologies for Adjusting to Alter

To successfully navigate the future of empathetic leadership, organizations must be proactive in preparing for and adapting to change. Here are a few methodologies for remaining ahead:

1. **Invest in Leadership Development**

Continually invest in leadership development programs that focus on empathetic skills, emotional intelligence, and emerging trends. This includes providing training, coaching, and opportunities for leaders to grow and adapt.

2. **Foster a Culture of Continuous Learning**

Encourage a culture of continuous learning and improvement. This includes remaining educated almost industry patterns, looking for input, and being open to modern thoughts and approaches.

3. **Adapt to Changing Expectations**

Stay attuned to evolving societal expectations and adapt organizational practices accordingly. This includes addressing issues related to DEI, corporate responsibility, and employee well-being.

4. **Leverage Technology Thoughtfully**

Use technology to enhance, not replace, human interactions. Ensure that digital tools and platforms support empathetic communication and collaboration.

5. **Engage with Diverse Stakeholders**

Actively engage with diverse stakeholders, including employees, customers, and communities, to understand their needs and expectations. This helps build stronger relationships and ensures that organizational practices align with stakeholder values.

Example: An organization might establish a task force to monitor and respond to changes in societal expectations and industry trends. The task force could provide recommendations for adapting leadership practices and organizational policies to meet evolving needs.

The future of empathetic leadership is shaped by global perspectives, technological advancements, and shifting societal expectations. By staying ahead of emerging trends and adapting to change, leaders can create a lasting impact and drive organizational success.

As we move forward, it is essential for leaders to remain committed to empathy, inclusivity, and continuous improvement. By fostering a culture of understanding, compassion, and connection, organizations can navigate the complexities of the future while maintaining a positive and supportive work environment.

CONCLUSION

EMBRACING THE POWER OF EMPATHETIC LEADERSHIP

As we conclude this exploration of empathetic leadership, it's clear that empathy is not just a soft skill but a fundamental driver of organizational success and human connection. Throughout this book, we have examined the profound impact that empathetic leadership can have on individuals, teams, and organizations. From fostering trust and collaboration to driving innovation and long-term success, empathy emerges as a cornerstone of effective leadership.

The Transformative Power of Empathy

Empathetic leadership transforms workplaces by creating environments where individuals feel valued, understood, and supported. Leaders who practice empathy build stronger relationships, enhance team cohesion, and cultivate a culture of mutual respect. This positive work environment not only boosts employee satisfaction and engagement but also contributes to higher levels of performance and productivity.

1. **Building Trust and Connection**: Empathy allows leaders to connect with their teams on a personal level, fostering trust and openness. When employees feel that their leaders understand and care about their well-being, they are more likely to be engaged and committed to their work.
2. **Enhancing Collaboration and Innovation**: Empathetic leaders create a safe space for team

members to share ideas, take risks, and collaborate. This environment encourages creativity and innovation, leading to more effective problem-solving and a competitive edge in the marketplace.
3. **Navigating Challenges with Compassion**: During times of crisis or change, empathetic leadership helps organizations navigate challenges with resilience and grace. Leaders who approach difficult situations with empathy maintain morale, address concerns, and guide their teams through adversity.
4. **Driving Long-Term Success**: The benefits of empathetic leadership extend beyond immediate outcomes. Organizations that prioritize empathy build stronger, more resilient teams, foster customer loyalty, and achieve sustainable success.

Creating a Legacy of Empathy

Creating a lasting legacy of empathy requires intentional effort and commitment. It involves embedding empathy into organizational values, developing future leaders, and continuously nurturing a culture of compassion. By focusing on mentorship, succession planning, and leadership development, organizations can ensure that empathetic practices are sustained and passed on to future generations.

1. **Mentorship**: Effective mentorship is a key driver of empathetic leadership. By modeling empathetic behavior and providing guidance, mentors help shape the next generation of leaders and reinforce the value of empathy within the organization.

2. **Succession Planning**: Identifying and developing potential leaders who demonstrate empathetic qualities is essential for ensuring continuity. Succession planning should include strategies for nurturing empathetic skills and aligning them with organizational goals.
3. **Leadership Development**: Leadership development programs play a crucial role in cultivating empathetic leaders. These programs should focus on building emotional intelligence, fostering inclusivity, and preparing leaders to navigate the complexities of the modern workplace.
4. **Organizational Values**: Embedding empathy into organizational values and practices ensures that it remains a core component of the company's culture. Leaders should communicate these values clearly, integrate them into policies, and celebrate empathetic behavior.

Embracing Future Trends

The future of empathetic leadership will be shaped by global perspectives, technological advancements, and evolving societal expectations. Leaders who stay informed about emerging trends and adapt their approach will be better positioned to create positive and impactful organizations.

1. **Global Perspectives**: As organizations operate in a globalized world, leaders must embrace cultural diversity and promote inclusivity. Understanding and respecting different cultural backgrounds will enhance collaboration and drive innovation.

2. **Technological Advancements**: While technology offers new opportunities for efficiency and connectivity, leaders must balance digital interactions with personal connections. Leveraging technology thoughtfully can enhance, rather than replace, empathetic communication.
3. **Societal Expectations**: Addressing societal expectations around corporate responsibility, sustainability, and social justice is essential. Leaders should align their actions with these expectations and prioritize employee well-being.
4. **Emerging Trends**: Trends such as purpose-driven leadership, emotional intelligence, and DEI initiatives are reshaping the leadership landscape. Leaders who embrace these trends will foster a more inclusive and supportive work environment.

Final Reflections

Empathetic leadership is not a destination but a continuous journey of growth, reflection, and adaptation. As leaders navigate the complexities of the modern workplace, the power of empathy will remain a guiding force, shaping their interactions, decisions, and impact. By embracing empathy as a core value and practice, leaders can create workplaces where individuals thrive, organizations succeed, and communities flourish.

In summary, empathetic leadership is a transformative force that enhances organizational culture, drives innovation, and fosters meaningful connections. As we look to the future, let us remain committed to leading with empathy, creating a legacy of compassion, and making a positive difference in the world. Through our actions and decisions, we have the opportunity to shape a future where empathy and understanding are at the heart of effective leadership and organizational success.

www.ingramcontent.com/pod-product-compliance
Lightning Source LLC
Chambersburg PA
CBHW050307230526
45471CB00005B/2056